THE FIVE

A RESEARCH-BASED MODEL FOR MAXIMIZING

COACHING

PEOPLE'S PERFORMANCE AND POTENTIAL

CONVERSATIONS

THE FIVE

A RESEARCH-BASED MODEL FOR MAXIMIZING

COACHING

PEOPLE'S PERFORMANCE AND POTENTIAL

CONVERSATIONS

JOHN GATES
MORGAN MASSIE
STEVE WILLIAMS

THE FIVE COACHING CONVERSATIONS

A Research Based Model for Maximizing People's Performance and Potential

Copyright© 2020 by

JOHN GATES
MORGAN MASSIE
and
STEVE WILLIAMS

All rights reserved. No part of this book may be reproduced or transmitted in any form or by any means, electronic or mechanical, including photo-copying, recording or by any information storage and retrieval system without written permission by the author, except for the inclusion of brief quotations in a book review.

ISBN # 978-1-7327738-2-0

Published by:
Avion Consulting Publications
4142 Adams Avenue, Suite #103-532
San Diego, CA 92116

www.avionconsulting.com

"Coaching is an interaction between two or more people, led by someone with content expertise and/or process skill, for the purpose of maximizing the performance and development of the coachee(s)."

~ AVION CONSULTING

Table of Contents

Acknowledgments IX
Introduction: What Is Coaching, Anyway? XV
  1. Challenging the Dominant Coaching Paradigm. 1
  2. Coaching and Adaptability 21
  3. Our Research Method. 33
  4. The Five Coaching Conversations Model 43
  5. The Coaching Context 57
  6. Coaching Cues. 81
  7. The EXPLAIN Coaching Conversation 93
  8. The EXPLORE Coaching Conversation 119
  9. The ENCOURAGE Coaching Conversation. 143
  10. The EMPOWER Coaching Conversation 169
  11. The ELEVATE Coaching Conversation 185
  12. The EVALUATE "Un-Coaching" Conversation. 201
  13. Coaching and Team Development. 211
  14. Conclusion: Get Talking, Get Coaching. 223
Bibliography. 235
About the Authors 241
About Avion 243
Index 245

Acknowledgments

IT TAKES A VILLAGE, AS THEY SAY. To all those who have contributed to this book and provided support along the way, we extend our sincere thanks.

We would like to thank our partners and colleagues at Avion Consulting for their support and advice: Jeff Graddy, Katie Keller, Sacha Lindekens, and especially Christi Smith, whose tremendous work ethic and attention to detail were invaluable qualities throughout the process of writing this book. And a special thank you to our Best-Coaches-Turned-Avion-Firm-Members, Darryl Albertson and Michelle DiTondo!

We would like to extend deep gratitude to our developmental editor Leslie Stephen, copy editor Linda O'Doughda, designer Tamara Parsons, and marketing professional Trish Keefer for their contributions and expertise throughout the process. We would not have crossed the finish line without you!

A special thank you goes out to numerous Avion Consulting clients who provided us with meaningful data through our interview and research process and graciously permitted us to reality-test our model with them, providing both feedback and validation along the way. Many thanks to our clients at AccentCare, AMERISAFE, Cubic Corporation, MGM Resorts International, and Welsh, Carson,

Anderson and Stowe. In addition, we want to thank Tyler Gates and Nicolai Mlodinow for research they contributed to this project.

To our Best Coaches who participated in our interview-based research, thank you for your time, your insight, and your meaningful contributions: Darryl Albertson, Hina Asad, Bruce Bochy, Keegan Bosier, Liz Brashears, Dr. Mark Brouker, Matt Cole, Tony De Nicola, Michelle DiTondo, Jessica Edwards, Jim Edwards, Ryan Fletcher, Dr. Kevin Freiberg, Cynthia Gentile, Dr. Marshall Goldsmith, Elisabet Hearn, Dr. Dilcie Perez, Garry Ridge, Debra Squyres, Alan Stein, Mike Twyman, Mary Watson, and Tina Whitaker.

To our colleagues outside Avion who continued to provide us with wise counsel and encouragement through the writing and publication of yet another book, we say thank you to Jeanmarie Alessi, Troy Blaser, Dr. Rob Fazio, Dr. Jackie Freiberg, Dr. Lisa Gates, Glade Holman, Netysha Santos, and especially John Stenbeck and Kevin and Jackie Freiberg, who continue to be great supporters of Avion Consulting and our efforts to put our own research and ideas out into the public sphere.

We would certainly be remiss if we didn't extend heartfelt thanks and gratitude to our families. To Lisa, Tyler, Cameron, and Lindsay; and to Don, Jasper, and Auralia. Thank you for your constant and unconditional love and support.

Last but certainly not least, we thank you, our readers, for your interest and desire to coach and develop others, while at the same time striving to fine tune the effectiveness of your own skills. Together we can make an impact on those we lead and coach by releasing ourselves from a self-limiting view of how to coach and leveraging a multi-dimensional approach that allows us to adapt our coaching approach in the moment based on the context and cues that present themselves. The outcome? For the people you coach – a more resonant coaching experience. And for you – satisfaction that you've achieved a deeper level of impact on their continued growth and development.

The Five Coaching

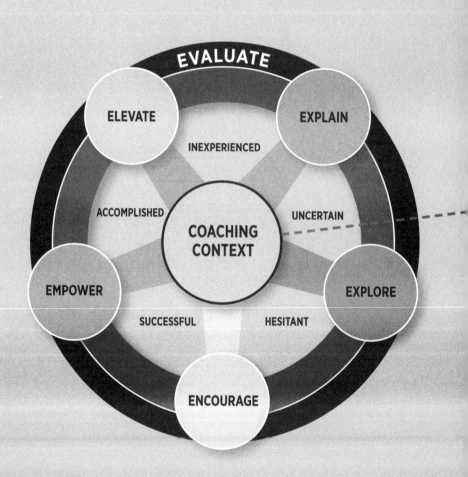

Conversations

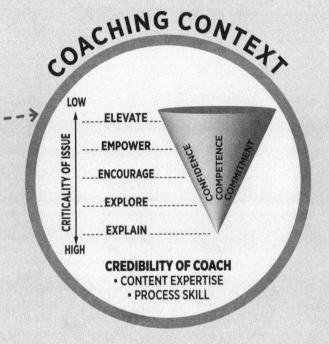

Introduction: What *Is* Coaching, Anyway?

> *"It ain't what you don't know that gets you into trouble. It's what you know for sure that just ain't so."*
>
> ~ MARK TWAIN - Author and humorist

WHAT IF THE THINGS WE KNOW FOR SURE ABOUT COACHING JUST AIN'T SO?

If you are reading this book, you are probably either an actual or an aspiring coach. And there is certainly no shortage of information out there intended to teach you what it means to coach someone, and how to do so effectively. Books and articles abound, and an entire industry of organizations that certify coaches in specific coaching methods has sprung up in recent years. But what if the dominant process being taught through these publications and certification programs does not really reflect how highly effective coaches actually coach?

That question is the starting place for everything in the pages that follow. And the reason we have the audacity to question prevailing wisdom in the area of coaching is that the book you have begun reading is not solely or even primarily based merely on our opinions about coaching, even though we collectively have several decades of experience coaching leaders. Rather, our audacity is based largely on research we did as a part of the writing of this book, research that took a few different forms (and which will be discussed in detail in Chapter 3).

In part, our research involved interviews with world-class coaches. Some of these coaches come from the world of sports, such as three-time World Series Champion Manager Bruce Bochy of the San Francisco Giants. Others are renowned coaches from the business world, such as Marshall Goldsmith, referred to by Fast Company as "America's preeminent executive coach" and widely cited by publications such as The Wall Street Journal, Forbes, and BusinessWeek as one of the world's leading executive educators.

In addition to interviewing coaches in various contexts who are widely and even publicly acknowledged to be at the top of their game, we also analyzed quantitative data that our firm, Avion Consulting, has on the nature of effective coaching. And then, once we had built a high-level model describing the practice of effective coaching, we used our data to identify and interview other great coaches from our client organizations – leaders who may not have the name recognition of a Bruce Bochy or a Marshall Goldsmith, but who nonetheless are great coaches.

And the bottom line is that we believe, based on both our research and our experience, that the dominant coaching paradigm these days may not be serving us well as coaches. So, the remainder of this book is devoted to offering a research-based approach to coaching that reflects what great coaches in a variety of contexts actually do. We call this approach our Five Coaching Conversations model, and at the heart of our book are five chapters that discuss in detail five distinct types of coaching interactions: The Explain, Explore, Encourage, Empower, and Elevate coaching conversations.

This Book's for You

We believe our Five Coaching Conversations model can be used in a wide variety of contexts – both professional and personal. However, as management consultants, we had three audiences particularly in mind as we wrote this book. We believe this book is especially for you if you are:

- A senior organizational decision maker or influencer who wants to implement an internal, organization-wide coaching practice that helps your leaders develop people and maximize their performance at all levels.

- An internal leader and/or coach wanting to expand beyond the theory and practice that dominate the field of coaching in the organizational context today and use new diagnostics and tools in order to maximize your effectiveness at coaching those you lead or support.

- An external coach (for example, a management consultant with a firm that offers leadership coaching as a service to your clients, or even a sole proprietor who specializes in coaching) who wants to expand and enhance your and/or your firm's coaching practice.

Now that you've identified which member of our audience you are – senior decision maker, internal leader/coach, or external coach – we'd like to tell you a brief story to illustrate why we think coaching is such an important topic right now for leaders in the organizational context.

Thanks to a mutual friend who made an introduction, one of us recently had lunch with Garry Ridge, president and CEO of WD-40. You are probably familiar with the company's flagship product, also named WD-40 – the extremely popular lubricant, rust-protector, and grease-eliminator. But you may not be aware that the company is also the maker of 3-in-1 Oil, Carpet Fresh, 2000 Flushes, and numerous other well-known household brands. And you may also be unaware that WD-40 is a highly successful publicly traded company and Wall Street darling, producing consistently strong financial results and shareholder returns.

> What if a great way for leaders to conceive of their role is, first and foremost, as coach?

Over lunch, our coauthor asked, "So, Garry, to what extent do you see yourself as a coach?" His reply: "That's *all* I do."

Now, perhaps there was a tiny bit of hyperbole in his response. After all, Garry is responsible for communicating the company's vision, ensuring its execution, driving results, maximizing employee engagement, leading change, and any number of other executive duties. However, we think his visceral response to the question is telling.

What if a great way for leaders to conceive of their role is, first and foremost, as coach? And what if, in doing so, they find they are able to maximize their effectiveness when it comes to virtually all other senior leader duties? We think this was Garry's point, and we believe it is a hugely helpful point of view from which you, likewise, can effectually lead anyone and anything from an individual employee to a small firm to a large global corporation.

Just how do we propose you become this sort of leader-coach? Read on!

Our Goal and Our Promise

We believe that in today's organizations, the concept and practice of coaching has morphed into something that is now pretty far removed from what successful coaches in a variety of fields actually do. Consequently, our goal is to offer a different way of thinking about coaching, and our promise is to identify a corresponding set of coaching skills that we believe will help coaches in virtually any context be effective and get the best possible results from their people. *The Five Coaching Conversations* is in part an attempt to reclaim the term "coaching" and talk about it in ways that high-performing coaches recognize.

The coaches and leaders we interviewed from multiple industries (we call them our Best Coaches) have utilized one or more of the Five Coaching Conversations to successfully build competence, explore options, restore confidence, motivate, and achieve impact with those they support. Their experience confirms – as did our parallel statistical analyses – a basic premise of this book: Effective coaching – that is, coaching that helps a coachee grow, develop, and perform to his or her potential – involves several different approaches.

As the book unfolds, we challenge the dominant coaching paradigm being promoted in organizations today, and we argue that coaching is a more fluid process than what is sometimes taught – a process that puts a premium on a coach's adaptability. We then describe the research behind our Five Coaching Conversations model, discuss the nature and importance of the Coaching Context, and identify a number of Coaching Cues that can help any coach determine the best coaching approach to use in a given context.

Several chapters are devoted to describing each of the Five Coaching Conversations in detail, followed by a discussion of what we call the "Un-Coaching Conversation." Finally, we explore ways in which our model is helpful, whether you are coaching an individual or an entire team, and we wrap up by outlining practical steps you can take to begin immediately applying what you have learned.

There are, of course, many other books and models out there that offer specific methods, frameworks, and tools to aid the coach in navigating the coaching journey. In fact, we have had extensive experience working with many such frameworks as leadership, team, and organizational development consultants, and we are fans of a number of them.

Our goal with this book is not primarily to discredit existing models but rather to extend on them by emphasizing the importance of staying focused on outcomes rather than process as a coach, and by being adept at using a range of coaching approaches, depending on the context. And, in doing so, we hope to offer a way of thinking about and practicing coaching that is reflective of how effective coaching is actually provided, both within and outside of the organizational context. Welcome to the journey!

Challenging the Dominant Coaching Paradigm

chapter 1

"I alone cannot change the world, but I can cast a stone across the waters to create many ripples."

~ MOTHER TERESA — Catholic nun and saint

WHILE THERE IS A LOT OF TALK ABOUT "COACHING" in organizations these days, that has not always been the case. Just a few decades ago, a "coach" was a person who worked with someone in a competitive endeavor, such as an athlete or a team of athletes. And the coach's primary goal, with the possible exception of coaches in youth sports, was almost invariably the same: To maximize the performance of the athlete or athletes the coach was working with. And ultimately, of course, *to win!*

And then people (mostly managers in organizations, human resources professionals, and management consultants like ourselves) realized that the role of a leader in an organization could be thought of as being, at least in part, like that of an actual coach. To begin with, leaders in organizations – like coaches in a sports context —

are responsible for maximizing the performance of the people they lead. And, at least in for-profit organizations (and arguably even in such not-for-profit contexts as higher education), the goal is, ultimately, to win; namely, to gain market share over competitors, to be ranked more highly than other organizations or institutions in the same field, and so on.

The comparison between "actual" coaches (such as the baseball, tennis, and wrestling coaches the three authors had when we were much younger) and "coaches" in organizations resulted in countless books, models, techniques, and consultants offering approaches to coaching in the organizational context. And as leadership and organizational development consultants ourselves, we have referred to these resources and used some of these approaches in our client work over the years – often with what we believe have been good results.

But there are a couple things we have noticed over the last several years about the way in which the nature of coaching has morphed in the organizational context. First, it seems to us that coaching has come to be known as a particular *approach* to interacting with people. True, different coaching experts have come up with their own models, which vary somewhat from one to the next. And true, the coaching experts who develop these models invariably stress that their models should be used flexibly rather than rigidly. However, these models all seem to be slightly different ways of describing the same basic *method* of interacting with the person who is being coached. We will say more about this a bit later.

The other thing we have noticed is that this basic method does not always seem to *look* very much like what actual, successful coaches do. And, perhaps more importantly for our purposes as coaches in the organizational context, this basic method does not always seem to *resonate* very well with actual managers and leaders we work with – people who are expected to be effective at coaching those whom they are responsible for leading.

The Nature and Impact of Coaching

All of this, of course, begs the question: What is coaching? A review of what has been written about coaching over the last decade or so reveals two key factors that characterize coaching: *Performance* and *potential.* Let's examine each of these factors more closely.

While practical experience and common sense suggest that good coaches help people *perform* at a higher level, the relationship between coaching and performance is nonetheless a widely researched question.

A great example of some statistically rigorous yet practical research on the relationship between coaching and performance comes from Google. In a July 2015 article published in the *Harvard Business Review*[1], David Garvin explains how a team of researchers within Google embarked on a project named Oxygen in order to answer the question: Do managers really matter within Google? Using sophisticated multivariate statistical techniques that even Google's skeptical, data-driven engineering types would respect, the Project Oxygen team arrived at several compelling conclusions, two of which we want to highlight.

First, they found relationships between the quality of managers within Google and important organizational outcomes such as

---

[1] Garvin, "How Google Sold Its Engineers." See the Bibliography for full details on publications referenced in footnotes and text.

employee retention, innovation, and other measures of performance at both the organizational and individual levels. Second, they identified eight key behaviors associated with Google's most effective managers. What behavior tops the list? Good coaching!

> "Effective managers impact performance... and coaching skills are key to managerial effectiveness."

Moreover, many if not most of the other eight behaviors that Google's most effective managers engage in, such as being result-oriented, sharing information, listening well, empowering people, and helping with career development, are clearly important coaching behaviors – at least the way we conceive of coaching. In short, the results of Google's Project Oxygen tell us two important things: First, that effective managers positively impact performance; and second, that coaching skills are key to managerial effectiveness.

Another excellent article on this subject was recently published in the *Journal of Positive Psychology*.[2] This research was a meta-analysis, meaning a review of multiple quantitative studies dealing with the question of the effectiveness of coaching in the organizational context, and the authors examined the effect of coaching on several outcomes, including performance. They noted that coaching does have a positive effect on performance as well as on people's well-being and attitudes toward work.

In short, we believe, and the evidence from these and many other studies shows, that there is a clear relationship between effective coaching and people's performance in a wide range of contexts.

---

[2] Theeboom, Beersma, and Van Vianen, "Does Coaching Work?"

> **ANOTHER IMPORTANT BUT MORE ACADEMIC STUDY** in this area was published in the *International Journal of Evidence Based Coaching and Mentoring*[3] (August 2009). Researchers Frode Moen and Einar Skaalvik of the Norwegian University of Science and Technology explored the effects of executive coaching on performance in their yearlong study of 144 executives and middle managers from a Fortune 500 company.
>
> Moen and Skaalvik found that there are, in fact, significant effects of external coaching on psychological variables that directly affect performance, including self-efficacy, goal setting, intrapersonal causal attributions of success, and self-determination.

The second key factor that characterizes coaching, beyond its relationship to *performance*, is that it has something to do with *potential*. Madeleine McNeely and Michelle Ehrenreich sum up the relationship between coaching and potential nicely in their Harvard.edu article, "How to Adopt a Coaching Mentality and Practice," stating that: "Leaders and coaches who adopt a coaching mentality and approach can help people realize their potential." These authors add that, "This investment will help retain top talent and foster a culture of growth and opportunity, which is a win for people and profit."[4]

---

[3] Moen and Skaalvik, "Effect from Executive Coaching."
[4] McNeely and Ehrenreich, "How to Adopt a Coaching Mentality and Practice."

Similarly, as John Zenger and Kathleen Stinnett put it in their book, *The Extraordinary Coach,* "If we look at the very definition of coaching, it is really about growing and developing other people."[5] In sum, a good coach will help others grow and develop, thus helping them achieve (or at least approach) their full potential.

Putting all of this together, we believe coaching, at its most basic level, involves helping people *develop their potential* in order to *maximize their performance* in one or more areas. And we suspect that most coaches, regardless of the context in which they coach, would agree that this is at least a directionally true statement about the nature of coaching.

The Dominant Coaching Paradigm

Closer scrutiny of the basic definition of coaching we have just offered, however, reveals one key distinction between our definition and what we believe is the dominant coaching paradigm, at least when it comes to coaching in the organizational context. Our basic definition is completely focused on *outcomes* (growth, development, maximizing potential, and performance) rather than *process* – meaning the specific approach taken by a coach. Many if not most other current coaching frameworks, in contrast, include both a reference to the *outcomes* in our definition, as well as some sort of stipulation regarding the proper sort of *process* that the coach should use.

A good and current example of this dominant coaching paradigm appears in a 2018 *Harvard Business Review* article written by Julia Milner and Trenton Milner.[6] The article is based on a study involving roughly 100 managers enrolled in a leadership training course. The participants were asked to coach one another on time manage-

---
[5] Zenger and Stinnett, *The Extraordinary Coach.*
[6] Milner and Milner, "Most Managers Don't Know How to Coach People."

ment, and the short coaching conversations were video recorded. The recorded coaching conversations were later evaluated by the participants and a panel of "18 coaching experts," all of whom had "a master's degree or graduate certificate in coaching."

In summing up the results, Milner and Milner state: "The biggest takeaway was the fact that, when initially asked to coach, many managers instead . . . *simply provided the other person with advice or a solution*" (italics added). They continued, "This kind of micromanaging-as-coaching was initially reinforced as good coaching practice by other research participants as well," explaining that "the evaluations peers gave one another were significantly higher than the evaluations from [the] experts."

Participants then received training in a set of coaching skills "based on the existing literature and our own practical experiences of coaching," and they had an opportunity to try out their newly developed coaching skills. And, perhaps not surprisingly, ratings of participants' coaching skills from the coaching "experts" improved significantly following the training.

Here's our interpretation of this study. Two experts in the field of coaching ask a group of managers to provide coaching. When the actual managers "provide advice," these two experts label it "micro-managing," even though the actual managers think it's pretty good coaching. Then, the two experts provide the actual managers with training in how to properly coach people, based on their experience and current literature in the field of coaching. Finally, they have the participants provide coaching the way they have been taught by the experts, and other experts who have been through coaching certification programs deem the managers to be more effective at coaching than they were before the training.

If nothing else, this article reflects the dominant paradigm in the field of coaching, which is to dismiss "providing advice" as simply "micro-managing" and to insist that true "coaching" involves a specific process (or particular set of skills) that is heavily focused on asking questions, listening, and "letting the coachee arrive at their own solution."

This article is not an isolated example. Consider Valerio Pascotto's article, "Why Coaching is a Necessary Leadership Style in a Matrix Organization," which appeared in *Forbes* on May 23, 2019.[7] For starters, just the title of this article illustrates an important part of the dominant paradigm, which is the idea that coaching is a particular approach (or, in Pascotto's words, a "leadership style").

Further, Pascotto (who is a member of the Forbes Coaches' Council) states: "A coach has a specific mindset that can be embraced by leaders. This mindset is one of trust in the resources of the colleague. The coach knows that there is a champion who can be awakened, affirmed and supported in the colleague. Such a mindset promotes a learning style rather than a teaching style, where the answer lies within the colleague as well as the pathway to solutions." As with the Milner and Milner article, and indeed as with most of the literature in the field of coaching, the key premise here is that "true coaching" involves drawing out answers that lie within a coachee.

Yet another example is reflected in the coaching model introduced in the book by Jack Zenger and Kathleen Stinnett cited earlier.[8] Now, we must note that Zenger is a management consultant whose

---

[7] Pascotto, "Why Coaching Is A Necessary Leadership Style."
[8] Zenger and Stinnet, *The Extraordinary Coach.*

work we have admired for years. Yet, consistent with the article by Milner and Milner, Zenger and Stinnett argue that "coaching is not about providing advice," but rather "most often is an opportunity for a leader to unleash the potential of her employees."[9] Before taking some exception to the perspective offered by Zenger and Stinnett, there are a couple of things that we find quite compelling about their point of view that we want to highlight.

For starters, they point out in several places throughout their book that they are not suggesting that coaches refrain from providing guidance altogether, an opinion we certainly agree with. In addition, we find it interesting that they refer to "unleashing the potential in people," an idea that dovetails perfectly with the mission statement of our own firm, Avion Consulting: "to partner with clients to unleash potential in people."

Having said that, there is clearly a very strong bias throughout Zenger and Stinnett's book toward the question-asking approach to coaching, a view consistent with most of the other current literature in the field of coaching (at least in the organizational context). Beyond promoting such an approach to coaching in general, Zenger and Stinnett also provide a specific model for having a coaching conversation. They use the acronym FUEL to represent four key steps in a coaching conversation: Frame the Conversation; Understand the Current State; Explore the Desired State; and Lay Out a Success Plan.

Interestingly, if you explore the specific guidance they offer regarding how a coach should handle each of these four steps in a coaching conversation[10], something becomes immediately clear: *Almost*

---

[9] Zenger and Stinnett, *The Extraordinary Coach*, 304.
[10] Zenger and Stinnett, *The Extraordinary Coach*, 564-566.

every example of communication they suggest is a question being asked by the coach!

A fourth example of today's dominant paradigm is the Integrative Coaching Model developed by Jonathan Passmore (2007).[11] This coaching model heavily focuses on the establishment and nurturing of a positive and productive coaching partnership, the idea being that the coachee can find solutions with proper forms of support and challenge from the coach. And, of course, the framework then includes a detailed process that essentially has the coach playing one particular type of role, that of a facilitator.

The Quintessential Example

Perhaps the best example of this idea that coaching inherently involves a certain or singular type of process is arguably the most popular coaching model being used today in the organizational context – the GROW model. While it's hard to determine exactly when and with whom this coaching approach originated, at least four people seem to have played a part in the development of this model: Graham Alexander[12], Alan Fine and Rebecca Merrill[13], and Sir John Whitmore[14].

As many readers of this book are probably aware, GROW is an acronym that stands for four steps in a coaching conversation: *Goal, Reality, Options,* and either *Will* or *Way Forward* (depending on which of the co-developers' versions of the model one is referring to). We believe GROW is a very useful framework for a coaching conversation, as it provides some structure for conducting it. The idea is that there are four questions that should be answered during a coaching

---

[11] Passmore, "An Integrative Model for Executive Coaching".
[12] Alexander, "Behavioural coaching—The GROW Model," 83–93.
[13] Fine and, *You Already Know How to Be Great.*
[14] Whitmore, *Coaching for Performance.*

conversation, and there is some logic in addressing these questions in the order of the GROW model – although, as its proponents are quick to point out, the approach should be used flexibly and not as a rigid, linear process.

Here's how the model works. First off, it's helpful for the coach to ask some variation of the question, "What is your goal here?" Presumably, if someone is getting coaching, there is some reason for it – likely in some way related to the coachee's performance and/or potential. So, it makes some sense to establish an actual goal for the coaching – in general, and/or as a product of a specific coaching session. In the organizational context, a general coaching goal might be "to help a leader successfully transition into a new role," while a more specific goal, for a given coaching session, might be "to help a leader effectively handle a performance issue he or she is currently dealing with."

Once a goal has been established, the next step in this framework is to address *Reality*. This has at least two connotations. First, what is the *current* reality? To stick with our second and more specific example above, regarding a performance issue, the point here might be to get clarity on exactly what the underperforming employee's current level of performance is, relative to some sort of performance standard. The second connotation of "reality" is reflected by the question, "How realistic is the goal established in step one?" In our example, it may be helpful to think through the question of whether it's even realistic to believe that the coachee is capable of achieving the expected performance standard.

The third step in a GROW coaching conversation begins with the coach asking something along the lines of, "What are some options here?" If a leader coaching an employee has thus far determined that the goal is to help the employee meet performance standards in one or more areas, gotten clarity on the employee's current level of performance relative to those standards, and determined that it is indeed realistic for the employee to at least meet the standards, then it makes sense at that point to identify a range of options that may get the job done.

Having done so, the final key question is, essentially, "What is your way forward?" (or, alternatively, "What will you do?"). After all, as noted earlier, the ultimate point of coaching in virtually any context is to help the coachee be more effective in one or more areas. This outcome, of course, is only possible if the coachee actually plans to do something specific to put the coaching into practice. So, helping coachees to determine not only what they *should* do, in theory, but what they *will* do, in actuality, is a key to improving performance in any context.

Again, we believe the GROW model to be a very sensible and useful approach to structuring a coaching conversation, and we ourselves have used it over time, often with good results. Here is our reservation about the GROW model – a reservation which, at least in part, represents the rationale for this book: A key premise behind this model is the assumption that each of its four steps should primarily take the form of questions that the coach asks the coachee.

Let us illustrate this in a few ways. We noted earlier that one of the people who can legitimately claim some authorship of this model is Alan Fine, an internationally renowned coach and founder of the consulting firm InsideOut Development. Fine outlines the GROW model in depth in his excellent book, *You Already Know How to Be Great*.[15] As the book's title suggests, the starting assumption for the

---
[15] Fine and Merrill, *You Already Know How to Be Great*.

coach is that "greatness" is already *within* the person being coached, so the function of the coach is to *draw that greatness out* — largely through highly effective question-asking.

Indeed, Fine argues that "many of us as coaches are still stuck in the story that telling people what to do will produce breakthrough results"[16]. He then makes the distinction between "Outside In" coaching, which primarily involves giving advice, and "Inside Out" coaching, which primarily involves questioning. And, of course, the basic assumption here – consistent with the dominant coaching paradigm today – is that true coaching is more "inside-out" than "outside-in." And that is the premise we want to push back on.

Challenging the Dominant Paradigm

Let us begin our challenge of the dominant coaching paradigm with a brief story. One of us has done a fair amount of work over the years with an intelligent, skilled, and effective consultant – one who was extensively trained in the GROW coaching method (and, more specifically, in the idea that the good coach is almost inherently a "question-asker" rather than a "statement-maker"). At the end of one day of work with this consultant, a day that our coauthor did not feel especially good about, our coauthor asked the other consultant, "How do you think the day went?" Almost reflexively, the other consultant went into "coach mode" and asked, "How do YOU think it went?"

Our coauthor's unspoken reaction was, *"Don't pull that coaching crap on me!"* He had already thought about the question, arrived at his own conclusions, and was asking a trusted colleague for *his* take because he *valued* it. In this case, the "question-asking" approach primarily had the effect of annoying the person who was essentially asking for some peer-coaching.

---
[16] Ibid., 72.

Another example of the limits of the dominant coaching paradigm really drives the point home (at least, it did for us). Two of us were recently doing some leadership development work with a consultant who has been steeped in the "question-asking" method of coaching, and the work involved, among many other things, a demonstration of what was intended to be an effective coaching conversation, with the other consultant serving as the coach. A slice of that mock conversation went something like this:

> **Coach:** So, what do you think you could do here?
>
> **Coachee:** Well, I think I could do X, Y, or Z
>
> **Coach:** Good – what else?
>
> **Coachee:** I'm sort of out of ideas – I'd welcome your thoughts
>
> **Coach:** No, really – what other ideas do you have?
>
> **Coachee:** Well, I've thought about it, and that's all I can think of
>
> **Coach:** I'm not going to let you off that easy – what else?
>
> **Coachee:** *"Now I'm just frustrated," he thinks*

Interestingly, a participant in the leadership development program (and, incidentally, one of the most senior people in the group and a very high-performing leader) later said to us, "If an actual leader in this organization were to approach a coaching conversation the way it was just demonstrated, it would fail miserably." It's in part because of experiences like this that we came to challenge what we believe is the dominant, question-oriented approach to coaching in the organizational context.

Put simply, we are challenging the dominant coaching paradigm because we believe that the insistence on defining "coaching" in the organizational context primarily if not exclusively as "structured question-asking" runs two risks. First, we believe it is inconsistent with what actual, highly effective coaches often do. And second, if we teach and train people who do coaching in the organizational context to over-rely on this method, it can both limit their effectiveness and diminish their credibility, as in the examples above.

To be sure, we are not the only people challenging the dominant coaching paradigm. In a recent Forbes article titled, "Coaching Isn't Just Asking Questions,"[17] author and leadership coach Carylynn Larson offers up the point of view that effective coaching includes a combination of both question-asking and sharing observations, feedback, and insights. As Larson puts it, "Sharing observations is the yin to the yang of coaching questions."

We agree; an effective coach must be able to effectively utilize multiple approaches within the fluidity of a coaching interaction, depending on what type of approach will work best in light of the coaching context. And yet, Larson's point that sharing observations is the "yin to the yang" of asking questions still understates the range of approaches that good coaches have at their disposal.

Best Coach Kevin Freiberg, best-selling author of eight award-winning books on leadership, put it well: "Being balanced and agnostic about what types of coaching you use is a more sophisticated and more elegant approach to helping people grow" than simply *asking good questions* (or, for that matter, primarily *giving advice,* or primarily using any other specific approach). We agree, and much of the rest of this book is devoted to offering a model of coaching that challenges the dominant, question-oriented approach to coaching,

---
[17] Larson, "Coaching Isn't Just Asking Questions."

and which offers any coach a way of being "balanced and agnostic" about the type of coaching that would be effective in a given context.

Having said that, we readily acknowledge that a tendency for a coach to over-rely on a "statement-making" approach to coaching is perhaps at least as inadvisable as a tendency to over-rely on a "question-asking" approach to coaching. And, further, we grant that some people are naturally wired to gravitate toward one approach over another (for example, giving advice when asking good questions to get the other person thinking through solutions would be more appropriate and effective).

In fact, one of the popular models in the field of leadership development, the Social Styles model developed by industrial psychologists David Merrill and Roger Reid[18], looks at people's behavior in social situations on two continua – one of which is whether an individual uses more of an "ask-oriented" or a "tell-oriented" approach to influencing others. And, in our experience, there are lots of highly effective leaders out there in each camp. The point is that effective coaching is not as simple as saying that "people tend to want to give advice; we need to stop that and ask good questions instead!"

So, it is not that we think the dominant paradigm is not a legitimate approach to coaching; rather, our position is that it is simply *one approach* to coaching, or one type of coaching conversation, and there are several others that are equally valid — depending on a number of factors that we will explore throughout this book.

---

[18] Merrill and Reid, *Personal Styles and Effective Performance.*

When we discussed our point of view on this with Best Coach Marshall Goldsmith, considered by many to be the world's preeminent executive coach, he said: "I completely agree with you; there's no research that shows that just asking lots of questions works." To illustrate, he noted that he is an expert in leadership, and he asked, "If I'm coaching a leader and he or she asks for my advice on something related to leadership, what am I supposed to do – start asking lots of questions?" He then argued that doing so would be like hiring a financial advisor and not expecting any advice on how to manage your finances.

Marshall's comment brought to mind the mock coaching conversation described earlier, so let's re-visit and tweak that exchange. Imagine a manager in a financial services firm having a coaching conversation with a new, junior employee – someone who is well educated but is in his or her first "real" job:

Coach: I need you to run a Discounted Cash Flow analysis

Coachee: (Not having been trained to do this): Uh, OK

Coach: So, how would you approach this?

Coachee: I really don't know – I haven't done one before

Coach: No, really – what ideas do you have?

Coachee: I honestly wouldn't even know how to start

> **Coach:** I'm not going to let you off that easy . . .
>
> Now, some might say, "Well, of course, the manager should provide some direction – but that isn't really a *coaching* conversation." To which we would reply – why not?
>
> This hypothetical and admittedly somewhat silly example gets at the heart of our point about taking an outcome-focused versus a process-focused approach to coaching. In this example, the junior employee is not very likely to "grow and develop" if the "coach" steadfastly refuses to explain how to do something that the employee plainly does not have any understanding of by sticking with an ineffective process (in this case, a question-asking approach). If we take a step back and think about the intended *outcome* of this conversation, is it not to help the employee perform the task at hand effectively, and to grow and develop in the process? In this case, the best way for the manager to "coach" the junior employee is to explain what a discounted cash flow (DCF) analysis is, and how to do this sort of analysis – much as a golf coach might explain to a new golfer how to properly grip a golf club.

In sum, based on our review of literature in the field of coaching, as well as interactions with many leadership coaches in recent years, we have reached the following conclusion: There is now so much emphasis on *not* giving advice when people are coaching that the pendulum has actually swung too far in the other direction. In other words, ironically, it seems that the exact opposite of what the various authors cited above have warned against is now true: Coaches are now extremely reluctant to ever give advice, *even when that's exactly what the person being coached is asking for and arguably needs in a given situation!*

This is the situation we are seeking to address with our research, our coaching model, and this book. And the next stop on this journey is a discussion of the relationship between coaching and adaptability.

Coaching and Adaptability

chapter
2

"The shoe that fits one person pinches another."

~ CARL JUNG – Psychiatrist and psychoanalyst

BY NOW YOU HAVE UNDOUBTEDLY GATHERED THAT OUR VIEW OF COACHING IS MORE *OUTCOME* BASED THAN *PROCESS* BASED. In other words, we do not view "coaching" primarily as "structured question-asking" – or as any other de facto method. Rather, we believe good coaching is whatever coaches do (within the bounds of what is legal, ethical, fundamentally respectful, etc.) in order to maximize the performance and growth of the person or people they are coaching.

Because countless approaches are available for you to use to maximize a coachee's performance, potential, and development, one essential quality you need to have is *adaptability*.

The Adaptability Mindset and Skillset

To have an "adaptability *mindset*" is to enter into any coaching conversation with the intellectual understanding and deep-seated belief that there is no one best approach to coaching; rather, effective coaches adapt their approach from one person to the next, and even with the same person from one context to the next.

To have an "adaptability *skillset*" means that you not only "get" that you must adapt your approach to the context; you also have the ability to actually do so effectively. And by "skillset" we literally mean a "set of skills." The various factors a coach should consider, as well as the types of behaviors in which a coach must be able to engage in order to effectively adapt, are wide-ranging and diverse. Let's explore a few prominent concepts that highlight the importance of adaptability as a key to effective coaching.

> **ADAPTABILITY MINDSET:**
> Involves believing that...
> - there is no one best approach to coaching
> - effective coaches adapt their approach from one person to the next
> - effective coaches adapt their approach with the same person from one context to the next
>
> **ADAPTABILITY SKILLSET:**
> Involves being able to effectively...
> - consider the various factors that make up a given coaching context
> - engage in behaviors that are likely to positively impact performance and development in that context

Personality Type and Adaptability

One variable a coach must be able to effectively adapt to is the personality of the coachee. Numerous models address personality types, among them the Big Five model developed by Robert McCrae and Paul Costa[19] and the Four Temperaments model developed

---
[19] McCrae and Costa, *Personality in Adulthood*.

by David Keirsey.[20] Arguably, however, the most popular of these models is the Myers-Briggs Type Indicator, or MBTI.[21]

As you are probably aware, the MBTI model consists of four dimensions (or "dichotomies") that get at a person's preferences: Extraversion/Introversion, Sensing/Intuition, Thinking/Feeling, and Judging/Perceiving. Without going into great detail, let us take one of these dichotomies to illustrate the importance – and, in many cases, the difficulty – of being adaptable as a coach.

Let's say you are coaching me, and I have a clear preference for "thinking" and "sensing." You, on the other hand, have a clear preference for "intuiting" and "feeling." As a result, your natural inclinations regarding how best to coach me may not hit the mark. You may be inclined to want to paint the big picture with me and to empathize with me regarding challenges I'm facing in pursuit of that big picture outcome. But I may actually desire coaching that helps me think through concrete, practical steps in order to achieve the desired outcome. Neither preference is any better or worse than the other; they are just radically different from one another. And so, a coach should have the insight to be able to understand what his or her natural preferences are, as well as the ability to flex his or her style in a way that will best resonate with the coachee.

Leadership Styles and Adaptability

As with personality types, numerous models address the reality that there are different leadership styles, and that it's important to adapt your style to the needs of the person you are seeking to influence.

---

[20] Keirsey and Bates, *Please Understand Me*.
[21] Myers and McCauley, *Manual: A Guide to the Development and Use of the Myers-Briggs Type Indicator*.

Among the more prominent of these models is Kurt Lewin's leadership style framework[22], which proposes three basic leadership styles: Authoritarian (autocratic), Participative (democratic), and Delegative (laissez-faire). Lewin's early work in the field of leadership set the stage for many subsequent models, and traces of his three basic leadership styles can be found throughout the leadership literature.

Another well-known model was developed by James MacGregor Burns[23] and includes two basic approaches to leadership: Transactional and Transformational. The former, as the name implies, essentially involves an exchange, meaning that a leader seeks to understand a follower's needs and then uses an approach to leadership that will meet those needs. The latter involves actually changing (or, more accurately, transforming) a follower's sense of what his or her true needs are, and then leading in such a way that higher-level needs and aspirations are met. Mahatma Gandhi was an archetypal transformational leader in that he helped to elevate an entire nation's sense of what their rights and possibilities were, and then he inspired that nation to achieve a vision based on people's heightened sense of those rights and possibilities.

Yet, as with the concept of personality type, one model related to leadership styles clearly stands out from the rest in terms of prominence: The Situational Leadership model developed in the late 1960s and presented in the book *Management of Organizational Behavior* by Paul Hersey and Ken Blanchard.[24] This model has been introduced to countless organizations over the nearly fifty years since its publication.

Situational Leadership is an approach to influence that involves four different leadership styles. The original names of the four styles

---

[22] Lewin, Lippitt, and White, "Patterns of Aggressive Behavior."
[23] Burns, *Leadership*.
[24] Hersey, Blanchard, and Johnson. *Management of Organizational Behavior.*

described by Hersey and Blanchard were Telling, Selling, Participating, and Delegating. As of this writing, the version of the model taught by the Ken Blanchard Companies uses the terms Directing, *Coaching,* Supporting, and Delegating (italics added). The "Coaching" style represents a particular approach to interacting with someone that focuses heavily on the coach asking good questions.

Although we define the term "coaching" differently from the Situational Leadership model, we do agree with the model's premise that adaptability is critically important any time a leader hopes to positively influence a follower. Indeed, one of our goals in writing *The Five Coaching Conversations* was to simultaneously support that basic premise while expanding upon the excellent work of Hersey and Blanchard. We seek to do so in several ways.

First, and most obviously, we refer to the interactions described throughout this book as types of "coaching conversations" rather than as "leadership styles." For us, this is not merely a matter of semantics. The terms "coach" and "coaching" have become ubiquitous in organizations since the publication of *Management of Organizational Behavior* many years ago. And, as we discussed earlier, we believe the dominant concept of coaching is now pretty far removed from what successful coaches in a variety of fields actually do. So, in this book we wish to reclaim the term "coaching" and discuss coaching practices in ways that high-performing coaches recognize.

Second, we propose five basic types of coaching conversations, whereas there are only four leadership styles in the Situational Leadership model. As anyone who has a deep understanding of the Situational Leadership model knows, the appropriate leadership style for a given situation, according to that model, is based on the "readiness level" or "development level" (depending on whether one is referring to the "Hersey version" or the "Blanchard version" of the model) of a "follower," and a follower's readiness/development level is "task-specific." In other words, since a follower may be at different "levels" for different "tasks," it's important to adapt your leadership style not only from one person to the next, but with the same person from one task to the next.

We believe all of this is true enough. However, having used the Situational Leadership model for many years (always with permission or certification), we have always been struck by how often people ask: **But aren't some people really at a pretty high readiness / development level in general?**

We think the answer to that question is: *Yes, absolutely!* In fact, most organizations these days have a name for such an employee: The "high-potential, high-performing" (or "hi-po") employee. And these employees require a whole different type of coaching – whether from a manager, an outside coach, or someone else. So, we are introducing a particular type of coaching conversation that we think is appropriate in this sort of context – the Elevate coaching conversation (which we discuss at length in Chapter 11).

A third way in which we seek to build on the work of Hersey and Blanchard is by broadening the concept of "readiness/development levels," referring instead to what we call the "coaching context." We believe that there are more factors that a coach needs to take into consideration than the two identified by Hersey and Blanchard (which are referred to using various terms, but which can be boiled down to the "ability" and "willingness" of a follower to perform a given task).

We acknowledge that this moves us away from a simple, formulaic way of assessing a situation in order to determine how best to adapt. However, we also believe that the way we characterize the Coaching Context in Chapter 5 adds some important shades of grey to take into account in order to maximize your effectiveness.

In sum, it would be disingenuous of us to not acknowledge that we studied Situational Leadership as graduate students, we have used it extensively as leadership development professionals, and we are fans of the model. At the same time, it's that extensive experience with the model that has allowed us to think long and hard about ways of building on it – we hope in ways that contribute to the field of leadership, team, and organizational development. In short, we believe having the ability to adapt your style to fit the development needs of the person you are coaching is one of the keys to effective coaching.

Emotional Intelligence and Adaptability

Yet another idea that gets at the nature and importance of adaptability is the concept of emotional intelligence. One of the early thinkers in this area was developmental psychologist and Harvard Graduate School of Education professor Howard Gardner, who argued that "intelligence" is not monolithic; rather, there are multiple forms of intelligence.[25] Psychologist and science journalist Daniel Goleman later popularized the term "emotional intelligence" in his book of the same name and in *Working with Emotional Intelligence*. More recently, clinical and industrial-organizational psychologist Travis Bradberry and his colleagues at TalentSmart have helped to make emotional intelligence an even more widely known and understood

---

[25] Gardner, *Frames of Mind*.

concept through a wide range of publications, including the popular book *Emotional Intelligence 2.0*.[26]

While there are many definitions of emotional intelligence, we believe that most of them have a few things in common. In essence, emotionally intelligent people

- **ARE SELF-AWARE.** In other words, they have a good sense of their own emotions and, in particular, the sorts of things that may "trigger" them.

- **ARE EFFECTIVE AT SELF-REGULATION.** When something "triggers" emotionally intelligent people, they are able to maintain "impulse control" and respond in an appropriate manner.

- **HAVE A KEEN SENSE OF OTHERS' EMOTIONS AND REACTIONS IN ANY GIVEN SITUATION.**

- **ARE (BASED ON THEIR ABILITY TO "READ" OTHERS WELL) EFFECTIVE AT ADAPTING THEIR OWN BEHAVIOR** in order to influence others. Or, as highly accomplished management consultant and executive coach Rob Fazio puts it,[27] they are effective at "reading" and then "leading" others.

For us, one of the most fascinating things about the literature in the area of emotional intelligence is the consistent research indicating that emotional intelligence is a better predictor of success among leaders in the organizational context than is either the traditional notion of intelligence (as measured by one's IQ) or technical expertise.[28] In short, it seems that leaders – including coaches – who are

---

[26] Bradberry and Greaves, *Emotional Intelligence 2.0*.
[27] Fazio, *Simple Is the New Smart*.
[28] Goleman, *Working with Emotional Intelligence*.

good at reading other people and situations, and then adapting appropriately and effectively, will get better results out of the people they lead than will leaders who are less capable in this area.

So, consistent with models related to personality types and leadership styles, the research in the area of emotional intelligence suggests that it is critically important to be able to adapt your coaching approach to the situation.

Adaptability in Action

To help bring the nature and importance of adaptability to life, let's consider a hypothetical example using the concept of emotional intelligence. Suppose a coach in the organizational context (whether an internal coach, an employee's manager, or a professional external coach) starts a coaching conversation with someone using the GROW coaching model, or some other, similar, question-oriented approach to coaching. And let's further suppose that the coachee starts giving off cues that he or she is not finding this approach helpful and is actually getting frustrated with the coaching conversation.

The coach who lacks emotional intelligence will simply forge ahead with the chosen approach, confident that the coaching model being used is the "right" way to coach others. Perhaps the coach is even somewhat oblivious to the impact that his or her behavior is having on the coachee. The emotionally intelligent coach, on the other hand, will be very attentive to the way in which the coaching approach is impacting the coachee. Further, such a coach will become aware of the cues exhibited by the coachee. If it seems that a given approach is not working well, the coach will adapt, moving, perhaps, to some other coaching strategy or, in our terminology, by changing to another basic type of "coaching conversation."

Of course, the way in which a coaching approach is making a coachee feel is not the only criterion for deciding whether that approach is appropriate. For example, you may need to use a very directive approach with a coachee who is underperforming and who has a blind spot with regard to her capability in the area in which she is struggling. She might feel uncomfortable in that moment, but it still may be the most appropriate approach. After all, as we often say to the leaders we work with, leadership is certainly not about making others feel warm and fuzzy all the time.

> **WE ARE SEEKING TO MAKE WHAT WE BELIEVE ARE THREE IMPORTANT POINTS HERE:**
>
> 1. Adaptability is essential to successful coaching.
> 2. The impact the coaching approach is having on a coachee is an important factor to consider in determining what the best approach may be in a given context.
> 3. If a given approach isn't working well, the effective coach is emotionally intelligent enough to realize that, and to adjust accordingly.

One Size Doesn't Fit All

"The shoe that fits one person pinches another." These words of Carl Jung with which we opened this chapter are a good reminder that when working with individuals, what fits one person may or may not fit another.

Placed in the context of coaching, this "rule" certainly applies. You most likely can recall a time when a leader attempted to use a "blanket" approach to coaching a team by tossing out general statements and tidbits of advice to the group as a whole. He might have had the best of intentions, but it left you and others scratching your heads and thinking, "He's not talking about me, is he?" Or, even worse, "I know who this applies to, and it's *not* me, so I'll just smile and nod and count the seconds until he steps down from his soapbox."

> *...it is important to consider the context in which coaching is taking place, including cues that the coachee may be presenting about what he or she needs in that context, and to use this knowledge to provide meaningful coaching.*

This can occur in one-on-one coaching as well, with the leader – again with the best of intentions – attempting to advise or direct a coachee through a challenge based on advice that worked for someone else in the past. The shoe just might not fit.

What's critical to realize in both of these situations is that doling out support and guidance can actually do more harm than good in the coaching relationship. At its best, it can fall flat and leave the coachee no better off than before; at its worst, it can hurt the credibility of the coach.

Continuing with our shoe theme, a better approach is for the coach to play the role of a cordwainer – that is, a shoemaker who makes new shoes, specifically from leather. When building a new pair of shoes, the cordwainer will consider the unique measurements, style, and other specifications needed to ensure the best fit for the customer. To extend this analogy to the practice of coaching, it is important to consider the context in which coaching is taking place, including cues that the coachee may be presenting about what he or she needs in that context, and to use this knowledge to provide meaningful coaching that *does* fit.

In short, there is no one best approach to coaching. Rather, we believe the effective coach must have both an adaptability *mindset* and an adaptability *skillset*. It was with this premise in mind that we began our own research into what effective coaches actually do and, based on our research, developed a model that we believe reflects the importance of adaptability in coaching, and also provides guidance on how to adapt your approach in order to ensure the best possible fit for a coachee in a given context. In the next chapter, we will discuss the method that we used for our research, and then we will follow with the model that came out of it.

Our Research Method

chapter 3

"Facts are stubborn things; and whatever may be our wishes, our inclinations, or the dictates of our passions, they cannot alter the state of facts and evidence."

~ JOHN ADAMS – 2nd US President

HAVING COACHED THOUSANDS OF LEADERS in many different industries in companies around the world, we have our own views of what "good coaching" looks like. And we readily acknowledge that this book represents in large part our collective perspective on that very matter. But we did not want our experience to be the *sole* basis of this book. Rather, we wanted to find out what good coaching looks like from actual good coaches – beyond just the three of us!

Sometimes in our field, researchers and authors gather data on an important question, and then they essentially go where the **data** leads them. That was the basic method of a previous book written by three Avion Consulting authors, titled *How Leaders Improve.*[29] In that book, the authors identified a sample of leaders who had

---
[29] Gates, Graddy, and Lindekens, *How Leaders Improve.*

actually improved over time, and then they asked the question: How did they improve?

In other words, rather than starting with a model or framework that explains "how leaders improve," they started more or less *tabula rasa* (Latin for "blank slate"). Then, based on structured interviews with a sample of leaders who had gotten significantly better over time, they identified themes and offered ten insights into how leaders improve.

> And we realized we might even find that the most widely used approach was indeed the Socratic (or question-asking) approach.

For the research project that resulted in this book, however, we did *not* start with a completely blank slate. Rather, we began with a basic premise, which is that there is no "one size fits all" approach to effective coaching. While at first glance this might seem to be an almost self-evidently true premise, as the first two chapters of this book argue, we believe that much of the existing literature on coaching, at least in the organizational context, to some extent flies in the face of this idea.

Based on this premise, we began our research with a tentative, high-level perspective of what different kinds of coaching conversations might involve. Then, we sought to do three things through our research.

First, we sought to either validate or invalidate our initial perspective. We went into our research open to the idea that we might well find that very accomplished coaches actually do use one basic approach to coaching others across all contexts. And we realized we might even find that the most widely used approach was indeed the Socratic (or question-asking) approach. On the other hand, we understood that we might find basic support for some version of the high-level model that we had developed at the outset of our data-gathering. (Spoiler alert – it was the latter!).

Second, to the extent that we found support for our basic coaching model, we wanted to use our research to essentially flesh out the model. For example, while we began our research with a hypothesis that, sometimes, good coaches really do use a largely one-way approach in order to explain things to their coachees, we wanted to learn from a sample of excellent coaches exactly what such a conversation might look like. What, for instance, are the different *types* of Explain Coaching Conversations?

Third, to the extent that our basic model was validated, and to the extent that we were able to actually flesh out the different types of coaching conversations based on input from actual, accomplished coaches, we also wanted to be able to illustrate the model with real-world examples. It's one thing to say, "Sometimes, great coaches explain to their coachees exactly how best to do something." It's quite another thing to add, "And here is an example of how an undeniably great coach used just such an approach."

So, having decided that we wanted this book to be based on new data in the area of coaching, and having also developed an initial hypothesis about what, in general terms, we might find, we needed to determine how our approach to data-gathering and data-analysis would work. Since the basic question we were trying to answer was, "What do actual, highly effective coaches do?" our immediate task was pretty straightforward: We needed to find some actual, highly effective coaches!

More specifically, when attempting to determine what good or great coaches do when they actually coach, we wanted to find people who: a) are recognized as exceptional coaches by those they coach; and/or b) have exceptional track records as coaches. We call these people our Best Coaches and will discuss each of these two types of "Best Coaches" in turn.

To identify members of the first group, we created a measure of coaching effectiveness, and then identified leaders who are especially strong at coaching based on that measure. For readers who are interested in this sort of thing, let us take a moment to explain how we approached this.

Our firm, Avion Consulting, partners with another great firm, Learning Bridge, for our survey and assessment work. When doing 360-degree feedback work, we often work with clients to custom-design instruments that are tailored to a given company's leadership competencies, organizational values, and so on.

Often, however, our clients prefer, for various reasons, to work with us using an existing 360-degree feedback instrument. When that's the case, the assessment we use most often is a Learning Bridge instrument called The Leadership Inventory. Because Avion has used that assessment in numerous engagements across multiple clients, we sought and received permission from five organizations to take the data collected with that instrument and use it for purposes of the study upon which this book is based.

To do this, a key question was: How can we determine, based on that data, which leaders are the Best Coaches in these client organizations? To answer that question, we used a statistical procedure called multiple regression analysis. For non-statistics types reading this book, that is an analysis that identifies key drivers or predictors of some important outcome. In this case, the important outcome (or "dependent variable") was Overall Coaching Effectiveness, and our measure of that was the item from the Learning Bridge Leadership Inventory: *"Provides useful feedback and coaching."*

Now, since our initial goal was to identify survey items from the assessment that are drivers of Overall Coaching Effectiveness, we ran our analysis and identified six key (or "statistically significant") predictors of that outcome variable. To once again wade into statistics-speak, those six survey items had a correlation (Multiple R) of .88, and Adjusted Variance Accounted For (Adjusted R Squared) of .76, or 76%.

Said another way, 76% of the variance in how people were rated on the survey item *"Provides useful feedback and coaching"* was attributed to how they were rated on these six items. Having an Adjusted R Squared of .76 is considered very strong and means that the items together contribute more variance accounted for than probability would randomly account for. In fact, 50% Variance Accounted for is generally considered strong, so 76% Adjusted Variance Accounted for is very strong. Simply put, the six survey items identified through this analysis as the top predictors of overall coaching effectiveness are, collectively, quite useful in determining who is actually providing good coaching.

All of this left us with a Coaching Index of survey items representing key behaviors that effective coaches engage in. The six survey items in our Coaching Index are:

- *Is selective in determining the issues on which to focus*
- *Sets clear performance expectations*

- *Encourages cooperative problem solving*
- *Celebrates current successes with those responsible*
- *Delegates responsibilities to those who are competent to handle them*
- *Demonstrates that he/she cares about the goals and aspirations of others*

The next step, of course, was to identify our Best Coaches using this Coaching Index. Using the above survey items, we ranked all feedback recipients at the five client organizations where we had data on those six survey items (101 in total) based on average ratings on the Coaching Index. We then selected the highest performing group (the top 25%) to interview about how they actually coach people.

Of the 25 people who made up our 360-based interview group, the demographics varied significantly: There are 15 women and nine men; four Human Resource professionals; a Corporate General Counsel; two business Presidents; a Head of Sales; and a smattering of other corporate roles. The mix is interesting, in that some of our Best Coaches have roles that would indicate they should be good at coaching (for example, human resources leadership roles), while others have roles that are focused primarily on P&L or other corporate responsibilities. So, one of our conclusions based just on our sample of Best Coaches is that good coaching is more a matter of the person caring about coaching and developing the skills to coach effectively than it is about having a job that necessarily and obviously requires good coaching skills.

The second group within our sample of Best Coaches is made up of people whose track records clearly demonstrate that they excel at coaching and have done so over time. Indeed, in some cases, people in this group get paid specifically to coach, either because it is part of their job descriptions, or because they personally identify coaching as being a key function, if not *the* key function, of their roles. In this group we have:

- **BRUCE BOCHY,** former Manager of the San Francisco Giants Major League Baseball team and winner of three World Series Championships

- **LIZ BRASHEARS,** Executive Director of Management and Leadership Development for TriNet

- **DR. MARK BROUKER,** United States Navy (Retired), former Chief Operating Officer for Navy Medicine West and former CEO of Naval Hospital, Bremerton, WA

- **TONY DE NICOLA,** President and Managing Partner of Welsh, Carson, Anderson & Stowe

- **MICHELLE DITONDO,** former Chief Human Resources Officer for MGM International

- **DR. KEVIN FREIBERG,** keynote speaker and best-selling author of eight award-winning books on leadership

- **DR. MARSHALL GOLDSMITH,** identified by Forbes as one of the world's five most respected executive coaches, and by the Wall Street Journal as one of the world's top ten executive educators

- **ELISABET HEARN,** CEO of Katapult Partners, a UK-based business and management consulting company, and multi-award-winning author

- **DR. DILCIE PEREZ,** VP of Student Services and Assistant Superintendent at Cerritos College

- **GARRY RIDGE,** CEO of WD-40, an internationally successful, publicly traded company
- **DEBRA SQUYRES,** VP of Customer Success at Beamery
- **ALAN STEIN, JR.,** professional coach to elite athletes including National Basketball Association star Kevin Durant

Regardless of which cohort a given interviewee was in, however, we asked the same basic interview questions:

1. Your title is (insert interviewee's job title). To what extent do you see yourself as a "coach" in your role? Can you please elaborate on your response?

2. What do you believe is the impact of effective coaching, provided by you and/or by others within your organization/team?

3. In what context would you coach somebody by explaining what you want the person to do, how you want him/her to do it, and so on? Can you provide a specific example of when you have used this coaching approach effectively?

4. In what context would you coach somebody by having a dialogue about some goal or issue, options for achieving the goal or addressing the issue, and so on? Can you provide a specific example of when you have used this coaching approach effectively?

5. In what context would you coach somebody by trying to motivate the person, build his/her confidence, and so on? What are some approaches to doing this sort of thing that you have found to be effective? Can you provide a specific example of when you have used this coaching approach effectively?

6. In what context do you believe the best approach to coaching involves giving the other person lots of latitude to approach a situation in the way that he or she thinks is best? Can you provide a specific example of when you have used this coaching approach effectively?

7. In what context would you coach somebody by trying to help the person think about things like professional aspirations, new challenges, ways of better leveraging strengths, work-related passions, and so on? Can you provide a specific example of when you have used this coaching approach effectively?

8. What else would you like us to know about what you think it means to be an effective coach?

For each question, we asked follow-up questions to probe deeper and to get at examples that reflect what our Best Coaches really do to help people grow, develop, and perform at a higher level, both on a given task or job, but also on possible future tasks or jobs. We then did a content analysis of the interview notes in order to: 1) identify distinct approaches to coaching; 2) validate (or invalidate) our initial, high-level coaching model; and 3) be able to provide details related to each approach to coaching so others can learn them and develop the necessary skills to apply them effectively.

Of course, the third objective would only be relevant if the second objective, related to validating our initial coaching model, was indeed accomplished. And the bottom line is that our Best Coaches did in fact indicate that they use a range of approaches when coaching others, and the range of approaches they described generally corresponded to our initial, high-level coaching model. In other words, our model was largely validated through our research. In the next chapter, we delve into The Five Coaching Conversations model in more detail.

The Five Coaching Conversations Model

chapter 4

> *"Making progress on longstanding challenges requires a different lens and a new approach."*
>
> ~ AYANNA PRESSLEY – US Representative

THUS FAR, WE HAVE PRIMARILY SOUGHT TO ESTABLISH THREE THINGS: First, that the dominant coaching paradigm in the organizational context today is primarily a question-asking approach; second, that rather than defaulting to any given approach to coaching, the effective coach must be adaptable; and third, that based on our research, there are five basic approaches to coaching that are effectively used by successful coaches. The terms we use for these five approaches are:

- Explain *New hire/new to industry*
- Explore *working together*
- Encourage *getting stuck/getting frustrated*
- Empower
- Elevate

By the end of this chapter, you will better understand how these five types of coaching conversations combine to form a coherent coaching model, as well as what each type of coaching conversation involves. Before delving further into our model, however, we think it's important to further discuss what we mean when we use the term "coaching."

Our Definition of Coaching

In the introduction to this book, we argued that, "coaching, at its most basic level, involves helping people *develop their potential* in order to *maximize their performance* in one or more areas." We then noted that while this view of leadership may seem pretty straightforward, it is different from most current perspectives on coaching in that its focus is purely on *outcomes* rather than on a particular *process or approach*. Because we are proposing a somewhat different and even contrarian perspective on the nature of coaching, we believe it's important to be as clear as possible about what we mean when we use the term. So, we would like to expand on the basic definition of coaching just reviewed and provide the following, more detailed one:

> *"Coaching is an interaction between two or more people, led by someone with content expertise and/or process skill, for the purpose of maximizing the performance and development of the coachee(s)."*

Because every term in this definition was chosen very deliberately, let us elaborate a bit on each one.

AN INTERACTION: Coaching involves some sort of interaction or communication; we like the phrase "coaching conversation" and will continue to use that term frequently throughout this book.

BETWEEN TWO OR MORE PEOPLE: For our purposes, we will generally assume that a coaching conversation is occurring between just two people; however, coaches clearly work with more than two people in many situations (think of a coach with a team).

LED BY SOMEONE: In order for an interaction to be a coaching conversation, one of the parties must be leading the interaction; otherwise, it's just a conversation.

WITH CONTENT EXPERTISE: Sometimes, the reason one person is in a position to be able to "lead" a coaching conversation is that he or she has some sort of relevant expertise that may be helpful.

AND/OR WITH PROCESS SKILL: In other cases, the reason one person is in a position to "lead" the coaching conversation is that he or she is skilled at the process of coaching.

FOR THE PURPOSE OF: Coaching is intentional in that it seeks specific outcomes; and even if it doesn't achieve them, it may still be coaching (just not effective coaching).

MAXIMIZING THE PERFORMANCE: One of the specific outcomes that a coaching conversation may seek to accomplish is to help the person being coached to perform at a high level in a given area.

AND DEVELOPMENT: True coaching is also intended to help people being coached to grow and develop, such that they are increasingly capable of performing well on their own, at increasingly complex work.

OF THE COACHEE(S): Throughout this book we use the term "coachee" to refer to anyone being coached.

As with the simpler definition of coaching offered earlier and reviewed above, this more thorough definition may seem to be just a variation of other existing definitions of coaching. However, as with the simpler definition, we believe the richer definition just outlined again distinguishes our notion of coaching from others, especially in the organizational context, in at least one important way: *There is no reference to the actual method of coaching.*

Rather, our definition emphasizes the *outcomes* of coaching: namely, the intention on the part of the coach to help maximize the performance and/or potential of the coachee. And if a coach manages to help a coachee arrive at one or both of these outcomes, then from our point of view, that is effective coaching . . . regardless of the method the coach uses. The following two case studies illustrate this point.

Two Case Studies

Our first case study involves the daughter of one of our coauthors, who played varsity volleyball for a high school team that was coached by a two-time U.S. Olympic medalist – a coach who had a track record of great success at another local high school for many years. At the first tournament where our coauthor had a chance to observe this highly successful coach in action, a player on his daughter's team served a ball into the net early in game one. The coach jumped up off the bench, yelled at the player, glared at her, and sat back down.

A little later, another player served into the net, and the coach again jumped up, yelled at the player, glared at her, and sat back down. Our coauthor, whose daughter was on the court and who would soon have her chance to serve, frankly did not particularly care for this coaching method at that moment!

However, neither of those players – nor any other players on the team – served into the net again for the remainder of the tournament. And the team won the tournament (which was a county-wide tournament featuring numerous powerhouse programs from volleyball-rich Southern California, by the way). Then the team ended up winning their conference that year – without losing a single *game* in conference play – an amazing accomplishment given that a match consists of the best three-out-of-five games. And our coauthor's daughter had one of the greatest experiences of her life over the course of that season.

It is probably safe to surmise that the reason the coach yelled and glared at players who served the ball into the net was that he had made very clear during practice that doing so was one type of mistake that was simply not acceptable on this team (the logic being that if a serve clears the net, the team that is serving at least has a chance of scoring a point on that play). This assumption is supported by the fact that there were other sorts of errors that did not prompt the same type of behavior on the part of the coach.

In short, it appeared that a part of this coach's approach to coaching was to make certain expectations extremely clear, and to let the players know in no uncertain terms that he was unhappy when they failed to meet those particular expectations. And, again, he was a highly effective coach who led his team to a championship.

Our point: What we *don't* want this book to be is a piece of work that causes actual, highly successful coaches in various fields to shake their heads and say, "That's a nice theory, but as an actual coach who has led actual coachees and/or teams to very high levels of performance, I can tell you that's not how it works in the real world."

Rather, we want this book to offer a perspective on coaching that is *informed* by such high-performing coaches, and which causes them to say, "Yes – you have captured in a very practical, user-friendly way the essence of effective coaching in the real world."

Now, some readers may at this point be thinking, "Ugh – I hope this isn't going to be one of those books that has lots of sports examples, but which doesn't reflect the way coaching works in other contexts." To which we would say two things. First, we want this book to resonate with coaches in a wide range of contexts, including business, sports, and others. And second, we think that coaching practices in the sports context actually do translate into the organizational context (among other reasons, many people in organizations played sports extensively while growing up so may relate and even respond well to coaching practices from that world).

Having said all that – here's a second case study, this one from the corporate context, to illustrate our point about being *outcome*-focused rather than *method*-focused. A leader in one of our client organizations shared an example of a very brief coaching interaction that certainly does not fit many notions of "effective coaching" in the organizational context, but which nonetheless was followed by a positive outcome.

Three people were riding a hotel elevator: The president of a company and two other fairly senior leaders. One of the senior leaders was about to give an important presentation in a conference room in the hotel. As the elevator approached the floor where the conference room was located, the president turned to the leader who was about to make the presentation and said, "Don't (expletive) up."

The third leader (the one who was *not* giving the presentation) later recounted that her reaction was to think, "You can't say that to him right before he goes on stage!" However, she also noted that the leader giving the presentation *absolutely nailed it!*

Now, we don't know for sure what the impact of the president's behavior was on the leader giving the presentation. Perhaps the presentation would have been even *more* successful if the president had not said something right beforehand that ran the risk of unsettling the leader who was about to take the stage in front of a large and apparently important audience.

> *Maybe he understood something about the mental toughness of the leader who was about to present. About his competitive nature. About the sort of "coaching" that would result in **focus** and **motivation** to excel.*

But maybe, just maybe, the president knew something. Maybe he understood something about the mental toughness of the leader who was about to present. About his competitive nature. About the sort of "coaching" that would result in *focus* and *motivation to excel.* Ultimately, the proof was in the pudding – the leader "nailed it."

Take our definition of "coaching" and apply every term to this example: "Coaching is an interaction between two or more people, led by someone with content expertise and/or process skill, for the purpose of maximizing the performance and development of the coachee(s)."

We believe that the interaction in the elevator described above, however brief it may have been, satisfies literally every word of our definition. And we are confident that many coaches who have actually coached individuals and teams to high levels of success can relate to this example more than they can to some of the very process-oriented, question-asking, G-rated, academically sensible approaches out there.

Now, please don't misunderstand us. We firmly believe that there absolutely are instances in which a process-oriented, question-asking, G-rated, academically sensible approach to coaching is exactly the right one to use! And, as leadership coaches ourselves, we often use an approach that can be described just that way. *But that's not what coaching inherently is.*

In the pages that follow, we will move from challenging the dominant paradigm and arguing that effective coaching is more about achieving a certain type of *outcome* rather than using a certain type of *approach*, to presenting our own model of coaching. And a good place to start is with the history of the term "coaching."

A Short History Lesson

Understanding the origins of the term "coach" will be helpful when it comes to understanding where our model – especially its graphic version, the Coaching Wheel discussed later in the chapter – comes from.

In fifteenth-century Hungary, the village of Kocs made a name for itself building carts and moving goods between Budapest and Vienna. Around that time, an anonymous carriage maker developed a much larger, more comfortable version of the common carriage, which was called a "wagon of Kocs," or *Kocsi szeter*. This term was later shortened to *kocsi*. The carriage was emulated throughout Europe over the next century and became increasingly popular as a method of transport. The term *kocsi* became kutsche in German, *coche* in French, and *coach* in English: "From the name of the English horse-drawn coach came all stagecoaches, motor coaches, and finally air coaches."[30]

The term "coach" as a verb was first coined by students to describe their tutors, because they comfortably and quickly got pupils to their goal of succeeding in their studies.[31] In athletics, team leaders were originally referred to as "coachers" until, in the late 1880s, "coaches" became the preferred term. In short, the modern coach is, in essence, a metaphor for the *kocsi* that served to get people from point A to point B in an effective, swift manner. The term "coaching" is now used as a popular term for helping people achieve whatever their goals may be, and it is used in many different contexts.

The Coaching Wheel

We chose to honor the origin of the word "coach" in the design of our model because we believe that maximizing the performance and potential of a coachee is a journey, with coaching essentially being the vehicle to aid someone in getting from point A to point B in their development efforts, much as the wheels on a motor coach aid passengers in getting to their destination.

As with navigating a vehicle on the road, there is one preferred direction to follow between point A and B: *Forward!* The places from which one may start (point A), however, are limitless, just as there are many possible destinations (point B). Moreover, we all know that on any given journey there will likely be diversions, and maybe even a U-turn or two. After navigating through the diversions (Roadside attraction! Pitstop! Flat tire! Oops, wrong turn!), hopefully the vehicle and its passengers get back on track, using the most direct and forward-moving route to the desired destination.

---
[30] Hendrickson, *Facts on File Encyclopedia of Word and Phrase Origins.*
[31] Ibid.

To that end, we visually display our Five Coaching Conversations as the five spokes of a wheel (see Figure 4.1), which demonstrates that there is no suggested "conversation number one" (point A) nor a "conversation number five" (point B). Instead, this graphic is meant to convey the idea that the coaching process is a fluid journey, with all conversations available to the coach at any time.

Figure 4.1 | *The Coaching Wheel*

Nevertheless, once a conversation has ended, there is a preferred forward-moving transition to the next conversation in sequence – consistent with the idea of a wheel moving in a clockwise manner. But it should also be noted that, based on cues presented by the coachee, it may be appropriate and even necessary for a coach to lead a coaching conversation in such a way that the coach and coachee are essentially in reverse (counterclockwise, as shown in Figure 4.2, right side) for some period of time. As we all know, sometimes in order to get to our destination, a U-turn is necessary! In Chapter 6 we will delve more into this notion that the type of conversation a coach should be leading, and even the direction of the conversation, should be based on what we refer to as the Coaching Cues that a given coachee is giving off.

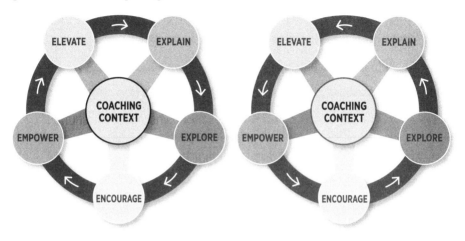

Figure 4.2 | *Forward and Backward Coaching Wheels*

At this point, we would like to point out one more important thing about our model. In Chapter 2 we mentioned that one of the methods used both to help validate our model and also to help us flesh the model out was a bit of quantitative research. Specifically, we used regression analysis to identify the survey items from our 360-degree feedback data set that were most predictive of overall coaching effectiveness.

We would like to return to that research in order to continue to explain how our model works – and, in particular, what each type of coaching conversation involves. Once again, here are five of the six survey items related to coaching behavior that were most predictive of overall coaching effectiveness – only, this time, with each item's association with our model:

- *Sets clear performance expectations* **(EXPLAIN)**
- *Encourages cooperative problem-solving* **(EXPLORE)**
- *Celebrates current successes with those responsible* **(ENCOURAGE)**
- *Delegates responsibilities to those who are competent to handle them* **(EMPOWER)**
- *Demonstrates that he/she cares about the goals and aspirations of others* **(ELEVATE)**

That these five items were all statistically significant predictors of overall coaching effectiveness, combined with the fact that each item above clearly corresponds to one of our Five Coaching Conversations, helps to validate our model. In short, when coaches are skilled at the practices outlined above, they are more likely to be perceived as effective coaches overall. Each of the five types of coaching conversations, represented by the five drivers of overall coaching effectiveness outlined above, will be addressed in turn in the coming chapters.

Beyond the five drivers or predictors of effective coaching outlined above, however, you may recall that there was actually a sixth survey item that surfaced in our research as a significant predictor of overall coaching effectiveness: *"Is selective in determining the issues on which to focus."* While this item does not clearly align with any of the Five Coaching Conversations, it nonetheless illustrates another important element of our model, and in fact is consistent with prior research conducted by and published in a previous book written by Avion Consulting.[32]

---

[32] Gates, Graddy, and Lindekens, *How Leaders Improve*.

Our firm's previous research found that leaders who improve significantly generally focus on what we refer to as a "Central Issue" when it comes to their efforts to get better. And, even though that research dealt specifically with what it takes to improve in the area of leadership, we think this idea that improvement efforts are more likely to be effective if there is some focus on a "Central Issue" applies to improvement efforts in general – including efforts in which someone is working with a coach. So, it's not surprising to us that another predictor of coaching effectiveness from our research for *this* book is that the skilled coach will help his or her coachee get focus on what he or she wants to work on. This additional, important coaching behavior is illustrated in Figure 4.3.

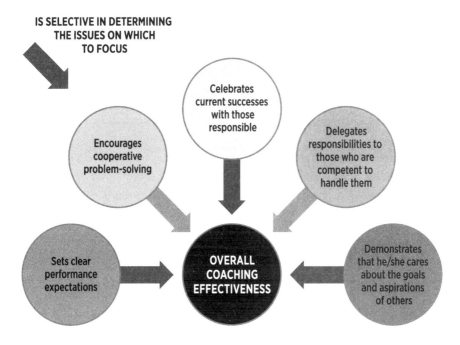

Figure 4.3 | *Coaching Index*

In other words, one of the things good coaches do is help coachees determine what they should be focusing on. Then, the key is for the coach to use an approach that will help the coachee develop and ultimately perform to his or her potential . . . in one or a select few areas at a time. In order for you as a coach to effectively do this, however, it's important to consider one more critical factor: What we refer to as the Coaching Context, which is the subject of our next chapter.

chapter 5

The Coaching Context

"For me, context is the key – from that comes the understanding of everything."

~ KENNETH NOLAND – Painter

COACHING ALWAYS HAPPENS WITHIN A CONTEXT, and the highly effective coach, first and foremost, has the ability to size up the context for a coaching conversation and then adapt appropriately. It seems that some coaches just have an innate ability to do this well, while others have to be more deliberate about considering the context. And, of course, by being deliberate about this over time, you will likely develop the ability to effectively factor the context into your coaching efforts. One way or another, however, awareness and consideration of context is critical.

Of course, the list of contextual factors to consider when coaching is endless. Based on our experience, though, five aspects of the coaching context are both important to consider as well as realistic to factor into your approach:

- The credibility of the coach
- The criticality of the issue

- The competence of the coachee
- The commitment of the coachee
- The confidence of the coachee

We will address each in turn.

Credibility of the Coach

Many of you are probably well acquainted with the American TV sitcom *The Office,* which had a good long run from 2005 to 2013. (Ricky Gervais's British version, upon which it was based, had a much shorter life span.) The show featured a manager named Michael Scott (played by the excellent comedic actor Steve Carell) whose fundamental issue was that his efforts to effectively manage (coach, motivate, guide, etc.) his team just never seemed to get any traction. In our opinion, one reason the show was so popular was that most of us can think of a manager like Michael Scott that we've had at some point in our careers.

The problem, of course, was not so much with Scott's methods themselves; rather, the problem was that his employees thought he was a schmuck. Or, in more technical terms, we would say that he lacked *credibility* in the minds of the people he was managing.

Credibility is a key to building a successful relationship between coach and coachee. We define "credibility" as "influence potential." In other words, the more "credible" we perceive some-

> *... the more "credible" we perceive someone to be, the more willing we are to be influenced by that person.*

one to be, the more willing we are to be influenced by that person. So, a person who is trying to coach you may be "doing all the right things" (such as offering explanations about how best to proceed, providing encouragement, or whatever else the context calls for), but you will likely be reluctant to really respond to the coaching if you think the coach lacks credibility.

So, what are the factors that account for a coach's credibility? There are numerous excellent sources on this topic, one of which is *Credibility: How Leaders Gain and Lose It, Why People Demand It.* In this book, authors Jim Kouzes and Barry Posner boil the essence of credibility down to the idea that you must "say what you mean and mean what you say." They go on to link the establishment of credibility to the practice of six key disciplines: Discovering yourself, appreciating constituents, affirming shared values, developing capacity, serving a purpose, and sustaining hope.

Another excellent resource on this topic comes from Harvard Business School professor Linda Hill, who writes in her *Harvard Business Review* article "Becoming the Boss" that many managers are not aware of the qualities that contribute to building credibility. Hill argues that people in leadership roles build their credibility as managers when they are able to demonstrate three strengths: Their character (the intention to do the right thing), their competence (both technical and nontechnical), and their influence (by creating a web of strong, interdependent relationships).

Largely consistent with the work of Kouzes and Posner, as well as that of Hill, our view is that the foundation of your credibility as a coach is comprised of two factors: Your *competence* and your *character* (see Figure 5.1).

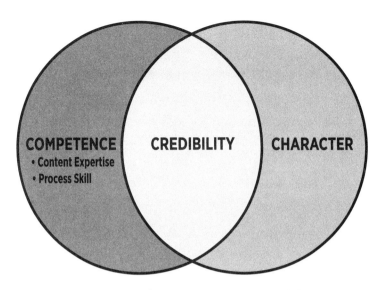

Figure 5.1 | *Avion Credibility Model*

Competence

One key aspect of credibility is "competence," which can mean lots of different things. For our purposes, we'll focus on two important forms of competence. The first type is knowledge or experience that is related to the area in which one seeks to coach others. For example, our consulting firm has worked with clients that have specified, when looking for an executive coach for one of their leaders, that the coach needed to have served in an executive role in a large organization at some point.

However, as anyone who has ever spent time in a Talent and Organizational Development (or similar) position in any organization can attest, if a requirement for being an executive coach was "experience in an executive role in a large organization," the pool of executive coaches out there would be . . . well, let's just say substantially smaller! But that is not to say that executive coaches who have not been actual executives themselves have nothing to offer. There is at least one other type of "competence" that we believe is a key aspect of a coach's credibility – and that is competence in terms of coaching skills. Which, of course, is what this book is all about.

In other words, if a coach (whether an external executive coach, a manager seeking to coach his or her employees, or any other type of coach) has a reputation for having helped coachees improve in terms of performance and/or development, then the coach may well be seen as highly credible – even if he or she has never actually "walked in the coachee's shoes," so to speak. Indeed, Best Coach Marshall Goldsmith, one of the world's most respected executive coaches, is the quintessential example of this. Similarly, a leader in a large organization may have credibility in his or her followers' eyes even without deep technical expertise in the particular group or function he or she is leading.

Here's an example. One of our financial services clients has a senior leader who has developed a reputation for being a highly credible coach. We have worked not only with this leader but also with people who report to her or have reported to her in the past. All evidence suggests that people generally really want to work for this woman in large part because she takes their development seriously, and she is constantly providing coaching that helps people take their performance to a higher level.

And here's the interesting thing about this leader. Over the course of her career in financial services, she has held at least three quite different types of senior positions: as a global functional head (multiple times, heading up different functions), as a regional head, and as a senior leader responsible for special projects within the Executive Office.

She is very smart, a fast learner, hardworking, and a person of integrity. Nevertheless, we believe that her success is due, in large part, to the fact that she possesses *great coaching skills*. So, for example, when she was appointed to head up human resources for her company – without ever having been in an HR role – she was still able to positively influence her employees (who had much more expertise in areas such as compensation and employee relations) in part because of her competence as a *coach*.

> *it's critically important to consistently act in ways that build trust with a coachee so that the coachee will be open to the range of types of coaching conversations*

In short, your credibility as a coach can be thought of as something that you *bring to a coaching conversation.* Put differently, if you are perceived as highly credible, then you stand a pretty good chance of being influential with the coachee . . . before you even start to have a coaching conversation!

Character

Character is relatively straightforward. A coach may be seen as being a person of strong "character" if he or she evidences qualities such as honesty and trustworthiness. Best Coach Dilcie Perez offered an interesting analogy related to this aspect of credibility. She told us that, in her experience, people will be receptive even to quite directive coaching "if it's grounded in trust," and she then likened the process of building trust to "making deposits in people's emotional bank accounts."

This analogy immediately resonated with us, as we have long compared building credibility with making deposits in one's "credibility bank account." In short, it's critically important to consistently act in ways that build trust with a coachee so that the coachee will be open to the range of types of coaching conversations you and the coachee may be having.

Criticality of the Issue

In the past, when considering the context to which a coach must adapt, we tended to focus mostly on factors related to the coachee (as we will discuss further in the next few sections of this chapter). However, we commonly hear from the leaders we work with that sometimes factors unrelated to the coachee must also be taken into consideration.

Perhaps foremost among such factors is what we refer to as the "criticality of the issue" at hand – for instance, the goal to be accomplished, the task to be completed, and so on. And for us, a good way to think of this contextual factor is to borrow from Stephen Covey, who noted in *The Seven Habits of Highly Effective People* that any given task or goal can be evaluated based on both its *urgency* and its *importance.*

Readers familiar with this work may recall that Covey referred to these two criteria in order to help us manage our time better. And while we think Covey's time management matrix is a great tool for helping employees maximize personal effectiveness, we are going in a different direction with these ideas.

We think the criticality of an issue on which you are trying to positively influence a coachee is an important contextual factor to consider, and we further believe that criticality refers to some combination of urgency and/or importance. The criticality of an issue, as just defined, may thus dictate what is likely to be the most effective approach to coaching someone. For example, it may make sense to have an Empower conversation with a more junior account manager who has been assigned to handle a meeting with a relatively small client, but for a large and strategically important client, it may be wise to either give the assignment to a more senior account manager or at least to offer some Explain coaching to the more junior person in advance.

Competence of the Coachee

The next three aspects of the Coaching Context all pertain to the coachee. And we'd like to start this section with a little context regarding where we first learned about the content of much of the remainder of this chapter.

One of us went to graduate school at the University of Southern California. While there, this coauthor took a course in the business school titled "Leadership in Organizations." To this day, it's the best learning experience he has ever had.

The course was taught by Dr. Steve Kerr, who later left USC to become the Chief Learning Officer of General Electric, and then served in a similar role at the investment banking powerhouse Goldman Sachs. In other words, Kerr was and is clearly a prominent and highly credible figure in the field of leadership development.

The thing that our coauthor most remembers about this class is that at the start of the first meeting, Kerr put a formula on the board, and said, essentially, "This formula represents much of what we are going to talk about over the course of the semester." The formula was:

$$A \times M = P$$

Kerr went on to explain that the "P" stands for "performance" – meaning the performance of the people that a leader seeks to lead. He then pointed out that the "A" and the "M" represent two factors that drive performance, meaning two things that one must have in order to perform well in a given area, and he asked the group of graduate students if anyone could guess what the "A" and the "M" stand for.

The answer was that "A" stands for one's "ability" to perform well in a given area, whereas "M" stands for one's "motivation" to do so. And the multiplication sign suggests that if someone is completely deficient with regards to one of these two factors, then there will be no performance – regardless of how great the value of the other factor is.

One reason this simple formula resonated so much with our coauthor and has stuck with him over time is that it seems to explain so much about what it takes to help people fully realize their potential. In other words, when you have the "coach" hat on and continue to focus on doing whatever it takes to maximize the "A" and the "M" of the person you are coaching, there's a pretty good chance that the person you are working with will perform well.

Indeed, a number of other thought leaders in the field of leadership have used similar terms (ability and willingness, for example) to get at basically the same idea. In fact, as noted above, the Situational Leadership model developed by Hersey and Blanchard decades ago introduced the term "readiness level" or "development level" (depending on which version of the model one is referring to) as shorthand for the combination of these two factors.[33]

---

[33] Hersey, Blanchard, and Johnson, Management of Organizational Behavior

Sometime later, Max Lansberg wrote a book called *The Tao of Coaching*, in which he used the terms "skill" and "will" to get at these same two basic factors. Regardless of the terminology, the idea, of course, is that it's important to adapt your approach when interacting with someone else for the purpose of helping to maximize his or her performance in a given area.

Getting back to the "A" in A x M = P, one aspect of the Coaching Context that every good coach must consider is the level of competence of the coachee on the issue at hand. Competence of any coachee simply refers to whether he or she has the knowledge, skill, and/or ability to perform the duty or to accomplish the goal. Sometimes competence is technical (for example, the ability to write code), and sometimes it's nontechnical (for example, the ability to manage conflict effectively in a team environment). Either way, however, one aspect of the Coaching Context that a good coach considers is the level of Competence of the coachee on the issue at hand. A lower level of Competence might require the coach to move toward the Explain or Explore conversations in our model, while a higher level of Competence might mean moving toward the Empower or Elevate conversations.

Commitment of the Coachee

While the Competence of the Coachee gets at the "Ability" aspect of Kerr's formula, the Commitment of the Coachee is one facet of Motivation. To flesh out the idea of a coachee's level of commitment, we'd like to look once again at one of our firm's earlier books, *How Leaders Improve*.

One of the ten insights into how leaders get better, based on the research that led to that book, was the "ripeness" of the leader. That concept was further explored by Jeff Graddy and Sacha Lindekens, two Avion Consulting colleagues, in their recent book *Ready, Set, RIPEN!* Based on the research underlying both books, we can determine someone's "ripeness" for improvement by evaluating five key factors that form the acronym RIPEN.

> **REALIZATION** means the person is at least *aware* that he or she should seek to improve in some area(s).
>
> **INCENTIVE** means the person sees some *benefit* of improving, or some negative consequence associated with *not* improving.
>
> **PRESSURE** means the person believes there is some sort of urgency that makes it important to improve *now*.
>
> **EXPECTATION** refers to a belief on the part of the person seeking to improve that he or she *can* get better.
>
> **NATURAL INCLINATION** deals with the reality that some people are simply more naturally predisposed than others to *want* to improve.

While the research that led to *How Leaders Improve* and *RIPEN* focused specifically on people in leadership roles, we think that "ripeness" is a concept that gets at the very heart of what it means for anyone to have a commitment to improve in a given area. In other words, we believe that these "ripeness factors" relate to the commitment of a coachee to improving – whether or not that coachee is in some sort of leadership role.

In order to be committed to improvement in some area, a coachee must first realize there is an area in which he or she should seek to improve. Otherwise, the coachee may have some sort of a blind spot. For example, many people we work with who request leadership coaching are seeking to improve in the area of communication effectiveness. And we often find that there are one or more areas related to the way in which they communicate that may be hindering their effectiveness, but about which they are unaware.

To illustrate, one of us was coaching a leader who was focusing on improving his communication effectiveness. In particular, a number of the people he worked with had expressed the opinion that he needed to be a better listener. This weakness manifested itself in his tendency to interrupt people. During one coaching conversation, the coach began to discuss this feedback with him, and as he was doing so, the coachee cut the coach off.

"Do you realize," asked the coach, "that we were talking about the fact that people think you tend to interrupt them, and as we were doing so, you interrupted me?"

"I did not!" he insisted. So, they continued their discussion, and sure enough, he once again interrupted the coach. When the coach once again pointed this out, he said, "Yes, I suppose I did, didn't I?" After a few more minutes, the coachee started to interrupt the coach once again. This time, however, he stopped himself and said, "I was just about to interrupt you, wasn't I?"

In other words, we are sometimes utterly oblivious to some behavior we are engaging in that is somehow hindering our effectiveness. Only when we are made aware of the behavior (perhaps by a coach who uses the Explain approach effectively to point out the behavior) can we potentially satisfy the *Realization* criterion for being ripe for improvement.

Although *Realization* may be a necessary condition for ripe not sufficient. If a well-intentioned and skilled coach helps a become aware of a behavior that is seen by some as less than ideal, but the coachee does not see it that way, he or she is still not ripe for improvement. In the example just cited, once the coachee realized that he had a tendency to interrupt, he immediately acknowledged both the drawback of that behavior (people feeling disrespected and not heard) as well as the benefit of improving (people would see him as a more respectful and skilled communicator).

Here's another example – this one illustrating a lack of *Incentive* to improve. One of us was coaching a leader who reported to an extremely senior person who was within a year or two of retiring. The senior leader had gotten to a point in his career where he was seen by some – including the leader our coauthor was coaching – as not taking certain duties very seriously, such as the way in which he planned for and then conducted himself in meetings for which he was responsible. The senior leader had a freewheeling style that some people saw as getting in the way of his effectiveness and, by extension, the effectiveness of his team.

Even though the senior leader had become fully aware of this perception through feedback from his direct report and others, he simply didn't seem to care. After all, he was extremely well-off financially, he would retire soon, and he had the age-old mentality that "you can't teach an old dog new tricks." In other words, he just didn't have any *Incentive* to improve. It was only when his direct report providing some "upward coaching" related to the legacy he was going to be leaving behind within his team did the senior leader really reflect on his incentive for improving in this area. And, indeed, the senior leader ended up being influenced by his direct report to make some improvements in this area.

A third "ripeness" factor that we think gets at the "commitment" of a coachee to improve is *Pressure* to improve. Once again, let us explain with an example.

One of us was asked to do a "leadership assessment" of, and provide some coaching to, a relatively senior leader who was transitioning into the role of managing a much larger division within the organization than he had been. The purpose of the assessment and coaching was to help the leader understand the strengths he brought to this new context as well as the potential pitfalls to be aware of. His manager (one of the most senior people in the company) had been the one to call for the assessment and coaching as part of his direct report's transition into the expanded role.

Interestingly, the senior manager had decided to have his direct report serve as a "co-head" of the larger division along with another leader at the same level. With two leaders now overseeing this large part of the organization, the coachee concluded (quite rightly, we believe) that his manager would be scrutinizing the relative performance of the two very closely.

The coachee in this example no doubt felt a healthy degree of *Pressure* to take any feedback he would be receiving via our coauthor seriously, to be open to the coaching, and to make sure that he was addressing any issues that surfaced through the process. In other words, he was ripe for, or committed to, improvement – not only philosophically or at some point in the future, but practically and immediately. Postscript to this story? That coachee became the sole leader of the division, and the other co-head moved on to another company.

And, finally, we think that the *Natural Inclination* ripeness factor also helps explain a coachee's commitment (or lack thereof) to improve.

The coachee who routinely seeks feedback, is open to feedback, earnestly tries to improve based on feedback, and places a true and high value on ongoing self-development is more likely than the average person to be committed to taking advantage of coaching overall, and not just in the specific area(s) in which he or she is receiving coaching.

Here's an example to illustrate this idea. Two of the coauthors have a mutual friend who is in his late fifties but who is as trim and fit as even the most well-conditioned twentysomethings. A competitive swimmer during his school days, he has taken up and excelled at competitive mountain biking, CrossFit, and other physically rigorous activities over the years. Recently, he learned about the benefits of a plant-based diet and is now following a disciplined diet free of any sort of meat.

Now, he is not a dabbler. Once he takes up a new practice in an effort to get his health and conditioning to a new level, he does his research, he experiments, he keeps what is working and discards the rest. As part of this new approach to optimal health, he is carefully monitoring outcomes such as the amount of time it is taking his body to recover from physically demanding workouts.

Our point here is that our friend has a *Natural Inclination* to improve — not just in the area of health and physical fitness but in general. So, if a very credible (competent and high character) coach in a gym or some other context were to offer our friend skillful coaching, we believe that he would accept because he is truly committed to putting new and compelling ideas into practice in a disciplined way.

In other words, if a coachee *realizes* he or she has one or more areas for improvement, sees some *incentive* for improving, feels some *pres-*

sure to improve in the short term, and is the sort of person who has a *natural inclination* to want to continuously self-develop, we would say that potential coachee is quite "ripe" for coaching. However, there is at least one more factor that must be considered: The *Expectation* on the part of coachee that he or she really can get better. And this factor from our RIPEN model pertains to the next aspect of the Coaching Context.

Confidence of the Coachee

A saying that is often used as a way of motivating people, but which we believe is demonstrably false, goes like this: "You can be anything you want to be" (or, its cousin, "You can do anything you put your mind to").

We don't mean to be curmudgeons or wet blankets here, nor do we mean to be so literal that we miss the larger inspirational point of these sayings. Yes, of course we agree that if people dream big and work hard, they have the capacity to do great things. Nevertheless, it's probably safe to say that none of us, the coauthors, will ever be a starting forward for the Golden State Warriors of the National Basketball Association, no matter how much we may want to be that very thing, and no matter how much we put our minds to it.

And we don't believe this is a trivial illustration. Coachees who have no *Expectation* that they can realistically improve in a given area are not truly ripe for coaching. And it may be that a coachee's lack of expectation that he or she really can accomplish something is well-founded, as in our example, or it may be that it is more rooted in self-doubt and other confidence-draining feelings and mindsets that may be artificially limiting potential.

Psychologists use the term "self-efficacy" to refer to a belief that sufficient effort, well-executed, will lead to successful outcomes. Individuals who lack self-efficacy, then, would hold the belief that even by being open to feedback and coaching, along with making concerted efforts to improve, the likelihood that they would actually improve is not that great. In other words, the coachee may be seen as lacking in *confidence* that performance at a high level in a given area is actually possible. As a result, he or she may not be especially receptive to coaching, at least initially.

This is not to say that the coachee who isn't confident is a "lost cause," any more than we are saying that anyone who initially lacks any of the *commitment*-related aspects of the Coaching Context is a lost cause. It's simply to say that the Coaching Context looks quite different depending on whether the coachee has high versus low confidence in his or her ability to excel in a given area.

Now, having discussed several aspects of the Coaching Context, let's put it all together. And, while we will offer a couple of analogies to help any coach quickly size up the context and determine the basic type of Coaching Conversation that is most likely to be effective in that context, we also want to acknowledge that, ultimately, it's a matter of the judgment of the coach – which itself is an idea we will seek to flesh out below.

The Context Cone

A simple analogy that we think can serve as a way for a coach to visualize several aspects of the Coaching Context and then at least approximate the coaching approach that is most likely to help a coachee perform well and develop is the analogy of a cone (Figure 5.2). Using this analogy, the basic idea is for the coach to get a general sense of where the coachee is at in terms of three of the five aspects of the Coaching Context – the coachee's Confidence, Competence, and Commitment with regards to a particular issue he or she is seeking to address with the help of some coaching.

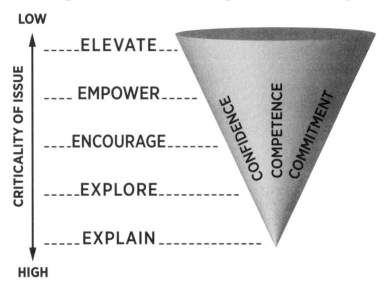

Insert Figure 5.2 | *The Context Cone*

Higher levels of these three factors can be thought of as greater amounts of some substance (water, sand, or even ice cream) filling up the cone. Thus, as the cone fills up, the coach should be adapting his or her coaching approach accordingly. Lower levels of Confidence, Competence, and/or Commitment would warrant use of more of an Explain or Explore approach, whereas higher levels would warrant more of an Empower or Elevate approach.

At the same time, and as discussed earlier, it's also important for both the coach and the coachee to keep in mind the Criticality of the issue at hand, which is represented by the continuum on the left side of Figure 5.2. Quite simply, if a given issue is highly critical, a coach may need to gravitate toward more of a hands-on, Explain-oriented coaching approach. Conversely, if a given issue is much less critical, it may be acceptable and even most appropriate for a coach to use a more hands-off, Empower-oriented coaching approach.

Of course, there is some tension between these various aspects of the Coaching Context. For example, if a coachee is pretty high in terms of Confidence, Competence, and Commitment but the issue is highly Critical, then the coach has a judgment call to make. But that's real life, isn't it?

And, of course, it's also important to keep in mind that all of this is ultimately dependent on the coachee's perceptions of the Credibility of the Coach, which we defined earlier as the combination of the coach's competence ("content expertise" and "process skill") and character. In other words, if a coach utterly lacks credibility in the eyes of a coachee, then regardless of whatever else may be going on, the context is not very conducive to a high-impact Coaching Conversation. We have put all of these aspects of the Coaching Context together in a single graphic (Figure 5.3).

Figure 5.3 | *The Coaching Context*

The Hub of the Wheel

The other analogy that we think will be helpful for the coach to keep in mind, in addition to the analogy of the Coaching Cone, is the idea that the entire Coaching Context can be thought of as the hub of the coaching wheel (Figure 5.4), and everything revolves around the hub. In other words, an effective Coaching Conversation involves the coach starting in the center of the model by reflecting on the five aspects of the Coaching Context (Credibility of Coach, Criticality of Issue, and Confidence, Competence, and Commitment of the Coachee), and then determining the basic sort of coaching conversation that is most likely to be effective in that context. As Figure 5.4 illustrates, the idea is to start with the hub and work your way out!

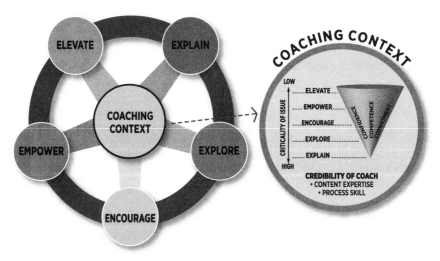

Figure 5.4 | *Coaching Wheel with Coaching Context*

Of course, while we hope this discussion and depiction of the Coaching Context is a helpful way of thinking about what the best coaching approach might be, we all know that real-life situations always involve many shades of grey. As much as we would like to offer an easy formula for deciding on the best type of Coaching Conversation to have, we think that in the end, a coach's ability to size up the Coaching Context and initiate and lead a Coaching Conversation that is a good fit for that context, depends on one key factor: Judgment.

Exercising Good Judgment

As we researched the behaviors that excellent coaches engage in and reflected at a deep level on the qualities that every good coach must have, we have come to the conclusion that much of this really does boil down to one essential: The exercise of good judgment. And what constitutes good judgment?

To gain insight into that important question, we asked ourselves: What sort of person might have some particular expertise in, and insight into, the area of *judgment?* The answer that came immediately to mind for one of our coauthors, perhaps not surprisingly, was: A judge! And, it just so happens that this coauthor's father is a *retired federal judge.* In fact, as luck would have it, several of this coauthor's family members have experience in the judicial system.

So, over a Thanksgiving dinner in the midst of the writing of this chapter, our coauthor posed the question of what constitutes good judgment, as well as the question of how to develop it, to her father the retired judge and other family members. Collectively, these family members offered the insight that good judgment requires *character, experience,* and *education,* but it often involves trial and error as well. As the retired judge (the coauthor's father) put it, "At some point, you have to make a decision and move on."

We couldn't agree more, especially considering the fluidity of a coaching conversation. Coaches are required to quickly assess the context, gather the relevant data, filter it through their experience and knowledge, and then act in the service of the person they are coaching. There is a danger of getting stuck in "analysis paralysis" if a coach dwells too long on the question of the optimal approach to take, which at best may cause an uncomfortable moment between the coach and the coachee, and at worst could harm the coach's credibility (especially with repeat offenses).

> Coaches are required to quickly assess the context, gather the relevant data, filter it through their experience and knowledge, and then act in the service of the person they are coaching.

Several of the aspects of good judgment that we have just discussed can be found in the following graphic (see Figure 5.5), which can be used as a self-assessment tool for people who find themselves in coaching roles and want to personally assess which aspects of "good judgment" they may naturally lean on and which aspects, if cultivated, could enhance their ability to demonstrate good judgment with their coachees.

Of course, there are countless other sources that one might refer to in order to better understand what "good judgment" involves, beyond even the very well-informed insights of family members. Interestingly, another personal experience of the same coauthor provides a thought-provoking way of looking at the complex phenomenon that we refer to as judgment. This coauthor once served in a leadership role for the Institute of Internal Auditors (IIA). Across the globe, IIA is the most widely recognized advocate, educator, and provider of standards, guidance, and internal audit certifications.

During her tenure, our coauthor led a team in the development of the IIA's first-ever online certification program, which involved

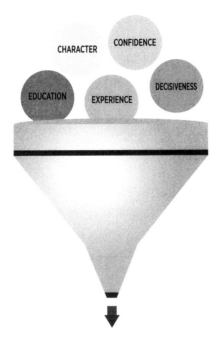

Figure 5.5 | *Judgment Framework*

attending and "auditing" existing classroom-based seminars and working with a team to redesign the content into web-based course format. Through this experience, our coauthor gleaned insights into the internal auditing role and process; the importance of making and the ability to make critical professional judgments in an objective, professionally skeptical manner was high on this list.

One online resource that auditors frequently refer to for best practices and guidance, called the "Center for Audit Quality," outlines a decision-making process to facilitate important auditing and accounting judgments in accordance with the competencies and ethics of the auditing role. While the process is specific to the auditing role, we recognize similarities to our own judgment framework. The elements of the effective judgment process for auditors include:

1. Identify and define the issue
2. Gather the facts and information and identify relevant literature
3. Perform the analysis and identify alternatives
4. Make the decision
5. Review and complete the documentation and rationale for the conclusion

When compared to our judgment framework, we see the most similarity in steps 1, 2, and 4 above. That is, the identification and definition of the issue most closely resembles our need as coaches to identify the cues that may present themselves during a coaching conversation; this leads to leveraging education, experience, and expert knowledge; all of which in turn leads to decisiveness.

Finally, we believe that confidence is a key aspect of all of this, meaning that once a coach tunes into the cues that may present themselves in a given context and factors in his or her relevant experience, the coach must then confidently lean into his or her character and be decisive about which coaching conversation to enter into with the coachee. As President Abraham Lincoln said, "Be sure to put your feet in the right place, then stand firm." And remember, you are doing so in the best interests of the person being coached!

Coaching Cues

chapter 6

> *"The most practical lesson ... [is] to observe."'*
>
> ~ FLORENCE NIGHTINGALE – English social reformer and founder of modern nursing

THE QUESTION THAT SURFACES NOW IS: How do you know when to transition from one coaching conversation to another (and in which direction on the Coaching Wheel – clockwise or counterclockwise, or even to one across the wheel entirely)? We aim to answer these questions by providing another layer of specificity and guidance on top of our wheel model: Coaching Cues.

One of us spent nearly a decade working with one of the nation's leading professional employer organizations, or PEO. During this time, our coauthor supported the development of leaders at all levels across the business and led a national team of talent development professionals in the creation and execution of a competency-based learning strategy.

During her tenure, our coauthor developed a Director in Training Program, which received a Learning Elite award from *Chief*

Learning Officer in 2015 (CLO Media.com) for content design and overall program success (85 percent of the program's graduates were promoted into leadership positions over a two-year period). Throughout the program, participants received informal coaching from both program facilitators and leadership sponsors in support of their development goals, with a more formal coaching option offered to graduates upon completing the program. The following case study underscores the value of both informal and formal coaching at critical points in a coachee's work life.

A Case Study on Coaching Cues

Oscar – not his real name – came into the program with a personal career goal on his development plan to step into a director role. Through program participation and coaching discussions, Oscar learned what it would take, step-by-step, to move into that position and then to perform the tasks and responsibilities of leading a team and an area of the business in the director role.

Oscar had many questions throughout the program, some of which was centered around the (natural) uncertainty he felt about the transition from individual contributor to people leader. This "cue" around uncertainty did not go unnoticed. Using the Explain Coaching Conversation, facilitators and leadership sponsors challenged Oscar to think through his own answers to such questions as:

- How will I build and empower a team?
- How will I redesign my relationships with colleagues who were once my peers and are now my direct reports?
- How will I balance the workload of my team?
- How will I engage remote employees?

- How will I delegate tasks to my team to keep my own workload balanced?

To help address the "newness" of the role, since this was a position Oscar was admittedly inexperienced in, coaching also entailed an *Explain* approach to enable Oscar to understand the tactical day to day "how-to's" inherent in the director role, giving him a "peek behind the curtain," as it were, to prepare him for that level of leadership.

After exploring different perspectives on being a Director, pondering and discussing "what-if" scenarios, and proposing potential ways to handle common people-leader interactions, Oscar finally arrived at graduation day. As part of the graduation process, each participant had a chance to sit down and revisit their initial development goals and reassess their current level of "readiness" to step into the director role, should an opportunity present itself. Oscar took a long, hard look at the year he had just dedicated to this program, at the knowledge he had gleaned on the "how-to's" of the role, and at the solutions he had proposed to prepare himself for common leadership challenges.

When it came to addressing the issue of "role readiness", Oscar had a breakthrough. After all the support, encouragement, and learning, as well as realizing what the role actually entailed, Oscar came to the realization that, although deeply grateful for the learning experience, he simply didn't have the desire to step into the director role as it was outlined at the time. He spoke candidly with the program facilitators and sponsors, who were all supportive of his decision. Oscar's personal career goal and desire had changed. And with that realization, the direction of his continued coaching changed to a conversation about identifying what the next career goal could be and providing him with the support and coaching to reach his newly defined path.

If coaching were a one-way journey with a one-way approach, program facilitators might have spent laborious and fruitless time in the next-in-clockwise-sequence coaching conversation in our model, *Encourage*, when Oscar announced his decision, in an effort to bolster his self-confidence by reassuring him that he had certainly demonstrated through his participation in the program that he was a strong, skilled and capable leader. Yet, in this case, no amount of encouragement or pushing would have changed Oscar's mind. Program facilitators and sponsors recognized that Oscar wanted to explore new options for other roles (leadership and otherwise) he might qualify for and, therefore, they made a "U-turn" at *Encourage* and went back to *Explaining* other options and *Exploring* the best fit. These continued conversations enabled Oscar to explore opportunities as they arose. Over time, he transitioned to a leadership role in alignment with his career and development goals and has since flourished.

> ...there are times when the best-suited coaching conversation is actually a step in the **counterclockwise** direction

As this example demonstrates, there are times when the best-suited coaching conversation is actually a step in the counterclockwise direction (Figure 6.1).

In our interviews with our Best Coaches, when we posed the question "How do you know which coaching conversation to use in a coaching interaction?" it became apparent that regardless of the coach's personal preference for a specific coaching model or methodology,

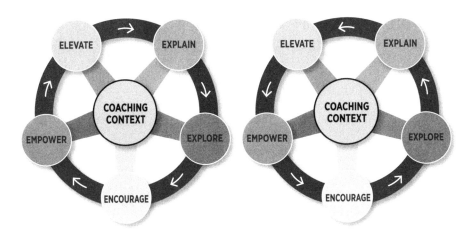

Figure 6.1 | *Forward and Backward Coaching Wheels*

they all agreed that coaching requires a certain level of competence in the area of active listening as well as situational awareness. As Best Coach Elisabet Hearn said, "The key to effective coaching is to just listen. In fact, try not to think at all! Listen to understand and not to respond. I've found that this approach gives me complete confidence. I will ask myself, what else can I ask to hear more?"

Another Best Coach, Tina Whitaker, Business Development Analyst at AMERISAFE, built on this thought. "I can tell which coaching conversation to use in a given coaching interaction by listening to the responses from the coachee. Simplified, if they don't get it, I step into an Explain approach. If they need to determine what resources are available to them, I switch to an Explore approach. If they can do something at about 80 percent capacity, it's time to Empower."

Through active listening, the coach can tune into certain Coaching Cues that come from the coachee. Such cues may be verbal or nonverbal signals and can aid the coach in determining which type of coaching conversation may resonate best with the coachee.

Matching Cues and Conversations

In this section, we outline a specific Coaching Cue for each of the Five Coaching Conversations in an effort to provide you with a framework that you can build upon with experience and practice. You'll see from Figure 6.2, Coaching Cues, that these include: Inexperienced, Uncertain, Hesitant, Successful, and Accomplished.

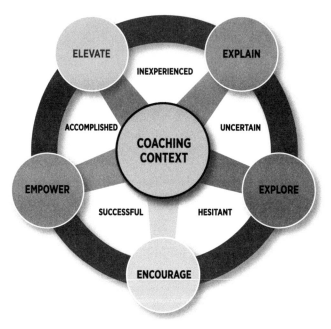

Figure 6.2 | *Coaching Cues*

Inexperienced: An EXPLAIN Coaching Cue

It's easy to see how the Explain Coaching Conversation can be used with coachees new to a role, when you are playing the role of mentor or teacher. In this situation, regardless of the coachee's prior experience and education, everything is "new" until the coachee grasps how to apply existing knowledge and skills to organization-specific processes and procedures. For example, Best Coach Debra Squyres told us, "When someone is early in their career and does not have a lot of context about the job, or if they are new to their role, then formal instruction may be needed." She cites the example of training someone on how to follow a process if the coachee is unfamiliar with the process.

What might not be as easy to see is the situation where a tenured coachee needs help handling a newly assigned task or navigating a new challenge. In these cases, the coachee's tenure or experience might lead the coach to assume that he or she should know what to do, but the truth is, there are times when even the most tenured, most experienced, and most educated people need support with a task or challenge they've never encountered before.

This "newness" is the cue that triggers the use of the Explain Coaching Conversation. It can be a new task, a new challenge, a new obstacle, or a new responsibility. Coachees facing one of these situations will benefit from the step-by-step, play-by-play, directive coaching that the Explain Coaching Conversation provides. More will be said about how to have an Explain conversation with an *inexperienced* coachee in Chapter 7.

Uncertain: An EXPLORE Coaching Cue

As Best Coach Tina Whitaker mentioned, "If an employee needs to explore what resources are available to them, I switch to an Explore approach." In a situation where the coachee *lacks certainty* about available resources, or shows uncertainty about the right combination of steps and the proper procedures to follow to complete a project, the coach would play the role of a sounding board and enter into an open-ended questioning approach to solicit two-way dialogue and explore what resources might be available or the necessary steps to take. More will be said in Chapter 8 about how to have an Explore conversation with an *uncertain* coachee.

Hesitant: An ENCOURAGE Coaching Cue

A coachee may be hesitant to take on some sort of challenge for a variety of reasons, but we think most of them fall into two basic categories: Lack of *confidence* or lack of *motivation*. In either case, it's time for the coach to have an Encourage Coaching Conversation with the coachee.

A coachee may understand *what* needs to be done and *how* to do it, but he or she feels hesitant because he or she hasn't actually *done* it before. Or perhaps the coachee attempted a task in the past and got a less-than-optimal outcome and so has received a bit of a blow to his or her confidence and needs some directed encouragement. In both of these situations—and there are undoubtedly many more examples—the presence of hesitancy paired with a general lack of confidence should cue you to put on your "coach as cheerleader/motivator" hat in order to help your coachee gain or regain the commitment and confidence to face the task or challenge.

In these types of Encourage conversations it can be helpful to imagine that with your words, support, and encouragement you are holding up a mirror to show others what they are capable of doing as they leverage their strengths to achieve what is important to them.

Best Coach Hina Asad offers this useful tidbit with regard to holding up the mirror with a coachee: "Tap into examples from successes they have had in the past and reflect back on these examples to help boost confidence."

Another Best Coach, Jessica Edwards, provides this example of coaching an employee who is feeling nervous about taking on an assignment: "I had an employee who attended a few job fairs as an observer. [The time came when we needed] her to take a more active role in an upcoming job fair. So, I approached her and said, 'You've been observing us for a while, and I think you can do this. How do you feel about it?' We had a discussion around her thoughts and concerns, and I reiterated my confidence in her ability. Fast-forward, she has successfully taken on the task on her own with no issue."

A second possible explanation for a coachee's hesitation is lack of motivation. Sometimes a coachee knows what needs to be done, and has actually done it successfully in the past, but now simply doesn't feel motivated to take on whatever the challenge is or to pursue it with maximum effort.

The senior leader in Chapter 5 who was responsible for a recurring meeting that was widely perceived as ineffective is a good example of lack of motivation. This leader had years of experience overseeing the team of people who participated in this recurring meeting, and he was generally considered an expert in the topics that the meeting involved.

He was also close to retirement and financially independent, and as a result, he was reluctant to do anything to substantially change the way he planned and ran the meeting. It was only after he was encouraged to look at the matter from a different perspective that he got past his reticence to change his approach to this responsibility. More will be said about how to have an Encourage Coaching Conversation with a *hesitant* coachee in Chapter 9.

Successful: An EMPOWER Coaching Cue

A coachee who has succeeded in facing a task, challenge, or obstacle will likely not benefit from a "hand-holding" type of coaching approach as much as he or she would benefit from receiving autonomy. In these situations, continuing to take a directive coaching approach will actually harm the coaching relationship and may come across as "micromanaging." Instead, providing a more "hands-off" approach and offering support and encouragement when requested is the best recipe. You can "cue" into this need for more autonomy by becoming aware of and celebrating successes with the coachee.

For example, our coauthor and a peer were getting ready to take the stage in front of a large group of finance leaders. The peer was asking specific and technical questions, trying to get answers to everything he might possibly encounter while on stage. Our coauthor believed this level of detail and specificity would only serve to cloud the peer's thinking and clarity while on stage and realized that the issue being expressed was actually a worry about whether he was fully ready to handle the situation.

Instead of responding to the peer's questions, he decided to be direct. *"You know this material, you know the audience, and you have the skill to do this, so don't play defense up there; instead, go on the attack."* This worked to help the peer shift his perspective. He was more confident in front of the group, which in turn let his personality come through, and, as a result, he was very successful in his presentation. You will find out more about how to have an Empower conversation with a *successful* coachee in Chapter 10.

Accomplished: An ELEVATE Coaching Cue

When the coachee has attained proficiency in a certain area by accomplishing incremental tasks and achieving multiple successes over a period of time, it's time to switch to an Elevate Coaching Conversation. (The key words here are "multiple successes," which distinguish the Elevate Coaching Conversation from the Empower Coaching Conversation.)

The Elevate conversation involves encouraging the coachee to take a more forward-thinking approach; the coach provides support for the coachee in articulating a vision and plan around what's next in his or her role and career and exploring the answers and options to the question that one of us often asks in jest, "What do you want to be when you grow up?" In the organizational context, the Elevate Coaching Conversation lends itself nicely to career development and career-path discussions when grooming high-potential employees for the next step in their career, or when positioning an employee or a leader to fill a role as part of the succession planning process. More will be said about how to have an Elevate conversation with an *accomplished* coachee in chapter 11.

Building Your Personal Repertoire of Coaching Cues

Through continued coaching practice, experienced coaches will undoubtedly begin to notice the Coaching Cues that coachees present in coaching interactions. Some of our Best Coaches have generalized these in terms that resonate personally with them, such as Tina Whitaker's summary earlier in this chapter: "... if they *don't get it*, I step into an Explain approach. If they *need resources*, I switch to an Explore approach. If they can do something *at about 80% capacity*, it's time to Empower."

In other words, to become a more effective coach, it is useful to build your own personal list of Coaching Cues, based on observations you've made over time. Doing so strengthens your credibility, expertise, and authenticity (or, to put it another way, your own coaching style). Best Coach Liz Brashears, Executive Director of

Leadership Development at TriNet, strongly believes in the value of developing your own coaching style. "Coaching is a journey, and the approach to coaching is not a one-size-fits all. What works best is to be authentically me: bringing a blend of my own experiences, my formal and informal training, my wisdom and my perspective, and weaving in a care for the whole person along the way. To me, this is the best recipe."

Now that we have introduced our Five Coaching Conversations model, explained the research behind the model, discussed the different aspects of the Coaching Context, and provided specific Coaching Cues associated with each type of Coaching Conversation, it is time to do a deep dive into each of the conversations. Each of the next five chapters deals with a different approach to coaching people, based on Avion Consulting's Five Coaching Conversations model. Let's dive in!

The EXPLAIN Coaching Conversation

chapter 7

"A leader is one who knows the way, goes the way, and shows the way."

~ JOHN C. MAXWELL – Author and speaker

A GREAT ILLUSTRATION OF THE EXPLAIN COACHING CONVERSATION comes from Best Coach Garry Ridge, CEO of WD-40, whom we introduced earlier. One of the fascinating things about the high-performing company that Garry leads is the degree to which they focus on their organizational culture. And the term they use to describe that culture is "tribe."

As Garry explains in his book, *Helping People Win at Work*, coauthored with Ken Blanchard, "To understand how a tribal culture impacts open communication, think about tribal leaders: They sit around a fire and *share their knowledge* with younger tribe members."[34] He goes on to make it clear: "That's the number-one responsibility of the WD-40 tribe – *to share knowledge* and encourage ongoing learning."[35]

In other words, sometimes certain people in an organization, or "tribe," have some sort of knowledge that others simply don't have.

---
[34] Ibid., 208.
[35] Ibid., 208.

The people at WD-40 with this special knowledge are known as tribal leaders. In our terminology, these people might simply be called coaches – regardless of whether they are junior or senior, internal or external. As we noted earlier, the thing that essentially positions someone as a coach is some combination of content expertise and/or process skill. That is, the coach knows something others don't! And, when that's the case, the best way to help the person being coached is to *share* that knowledge or expertise. In a word, to *Explain*.

To borrow an example from the culinary world, if you want to learn how to prepare French food, you need to learn proper knife skills. This means, in part, understanding the correct knives to use and how to chop, slice, and mince with them. It would be more effective for an aspiring French chef to learn the difference between julienned and brunoised vegetables from a thorough explanation of those techniques by an expert rather than by being questioned on their textbook knowledge.

Yet, while there are clearly times to simply explain to someone what should be done and how it should be done, when coaches in the organizational context use this approach, it often conjures up images of micromanagement and condescending interactions. To dispel that notion, let's look at an example of a context in which a coach *should* have used an Explain approach but did not – with less than optimal results.

A Missed Opportunity to Explain

Luke's company was preparing for a high-stakes, public earnings call with the company analysts. In a situation like this it's critical that information be communicated clearly and strategically, not least because the calls are recorded and can have significant repercussions. Luke, the company's senior business development person, was rarely involved in the financial side of the company. He was asked to participate in the earnings call for the first time.

When it was his turn to speak, Luke misspoke and volunteered information he should not have disclosed publicly. His team quickly started giving him nonverbal signals to stop talking. Growing more nervous, however, he continued to speak, making things worse. His whole group jumped in to try to salvage the call, but, needless to say, this episode ended up making the company look bad.

You can see why this happened, right? Luke's manager and other company leaders assumed that, because he was a high-level employee and a competent person in other areas, he would therefore be capable in the context at hand. Because they knew him to be credible in one area, business development, they attributed that same credibility to him in this situation when they should not have.

Luke was smart and capable, yes, but because this was a situation he had not been involved in before, he needed coaching. If somebody had taken the time to teach him the proper guidelines in the earnings call context, or even asked him how comfortable he was in that context, the bad scene might have been avoided. Luke's manager might not have adequately prepared him because of a reluctance to seem condescending, or perhaps he thought such a conversation was being redundant, or something else along those lines. The failure to Explain, however, caused an embarrassing situation, and even created some risk for the company in light of the fact that statements made during earnings calls may actually have legal consequences.

What the Explain Coaching Conversation Involves

Let's turn our attention to what the Explain Coaching Conversation actually involves when it is used in the right type of context, and with skill on the part of the coach. To begin this discussion, let us briefly touch on the way in which this type of conversation is typically characterized by other thought leaders in the field of coaching in the organizational context.

One of our issues with the way in which coach-directed communication is described in the coaching literature is that it is sometimes presented as easy, simplistic, and/or unidimensional. For example, Jack Zenger and Kathleen Stinnett repeatedly refer to coach-directed communication as "giving advice," and claim that, "By offering advice, we are essentially offering our version of fish to our colleagues" (a reference, of course, to Confucius' saying, *"Give a man a fish and you'll feed him for a day; teach a man to fish, and you'll feed him for a lifetime"*). Zenger and Stinnet continue, saying that, "By coaching instead, we will help grow the capacity of our colleagues, so that they can determine their own best actions to take."[36]

> *"By coaching, we will help grow the capacity of our colleagues, so that they can determine their own best actions to take."*

We find two things to be noteworthy about Zenger and Stinnet's view here. First, consistent with what we discussed in Chapter 1, it is interesting that these authors contrast "offering advice" with

---
[36] Zenger and Stinnett, *The Extraordinary Coach*, 156-157

"coaching," whereas we believe that "offering advice" is actually a form of communication that falls *within* the realm of coaching.

Second, Zenger and Stinnett seem to suggest that coach-directed communication and "offering advice" are essentially one-and-the-same, whereas we would claim that "offering advice" is actually one of *several* different types of coach-directed communication – all of which may be useful and appropriate types of coaching.

Now, in fairness, we must acknowledge that Zenger and Stinnett allow that "clearly, advice has its time and place – it just happens to be much later and more infrequently than you may currently be thinking."[37] They continue, "Most often the successes occur when one person has specifically asked for advice."[38]

Our view, on the other hand, is that advice-giving, and an Explain approach to coaching more broadly, is a critical tool in the coach's toolkit, one that is on par with every other tool in terms of its potential value – when used *effectively* and in the *right Coaching Context*. Indeed, we use the term "Explain" to encompass all the various forms of coach-directed coaching illustrated in Figure 7.1, which include:

- Offering advice
- Providing vision
- Stating expectations
- Sharing experience (or expertise)
- Giving direction
- Giving feedback

---

[37] Zenger and Stinnett, *The Extraordinary Coach*, 133
[38] Ibid., 133.

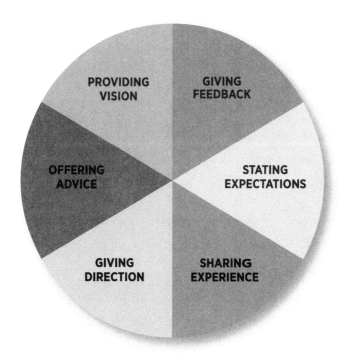

Figure 7.1 | *What Explain Includes*

Offering Advice

As stated above, we readily acknowledge that offering advice is at least one valid form of an Explain Coaching Conversation, so we've chosen to start there. And, to do so, we'd like to offer a personal example.

One of us used to serve a client that always hosted a golf outing as a part of a particular, recurring engagement with them. The invitation also included the option to work with a golf pro before the actual round of golf.

Despite having played many rounds of golf during his life, our coauthor had never become a very good golfer. And, while he was acutely aware of some of his problems (such as a chronic slice when hitting tee shots), he had struggled for years to truly understand the causes of his problems in order to be able to correct them.

During one engagement with this client, he had an opportunity to work for an hour with a golf pro at the highly regarded Las Colinas golf course just outside of Dallas, Texas. The pro studied our coauthor's swing for a few minutes and then offered two specific pieces of advice. "Focus on keeping your weight on the balls of your feet," he said, and then he offered similarly specific advice regarding the backswing.

Our coauthor then hit as beautiful a golf shot as he had ever hit, followed by another, then another. He then went out with a foursome – including three people from the client organization – and played the best round of golf he had ever played. The golf pro, by giving him a couple of bits of expert advice, was able to immediately improve our coauthor's performance (and, incidentally, his enjoyment of the game) if only for one brief, fleeting afternoon.

Now, suppose the coach in this example had gone into the golf lesson firmly subscribing to the adage, "I should refrain from giving advice; I will better grow this golfer's capacity if I allow him to determine the best course of action to take." It would have resulted in a ridiculous scene in which the expert coach is looking at the struggling golfer's swing, understanding with near certainty exactly what the issue is, but not saying so because giving advice is not what good coaches do!

Those expert and well-articulated pieces of advice were appropriate, and in our opinion, they certainly qualify as good coaching. Some people might maintain, however, "That's not the same as what we mean by coaching in the *organizational* setting!" To which we would ask: Why not?

To illustrate the idea that giving advice is a perfectly valid coaching approach in the *organizational* context, here's a work-related example. Best Coach Dr. Mark Brouker held numerous senior leadership positions during his career as an officer in the US Navy, including CEO of the Naval Hospital in Bremerton, Washington, and then COO of Navy Medicine West, overseeing all ten naval hospitals from the West Coast of the United States to the Indian Ocean.

When Mark was COO, one of the CEOs reporting to him put in a request for funding new headcount that was significantly greater than what any of the other nine CEOs were requesting. Mark had to review each request before ultimately sending it to Washington, DC, for approval, and he realized that this particular request would not only be rejected, it would also reflect unfavorably on the CEO making the request. Mark saw a "coaching moment." But rather than trying to get the CEO to arrive at the conclusion that he should reduce the amount of his budget request by asking good questions, such as "What do you think the impact of proceeding with this request might be?", Mark chose a more direct approach.

As Mark tells the story, he called up the CEO and said, "Hey, you may want to rethink this budget request," and then proceeded to provide the rationale behind this advice, explaining that a request so large and out of whack with what the other CEOs were requesting would likely result in Washington higher-ups putting the CEO under a microscope – inviting more scrutiny than he might want from on-high.

Two other aspects of this story illustrate elements of the importance of sizing up the Coaching Context. First, the ultimate decision makers in Washington were pressing for the numbers, so there was some urgency to this issue. Second, Mark emphasized that "this CEO trusted me," which is another way of saying he had credibility in the eyes of the CEO.

Because Mark had the competence to know that something a direct report wanted to do would be a poor decision, because the situation was urgent, and because Mark's credibility was strong, a very direct Explain conversation was appropriate and helpful. This is an example of an effective coaching conversation in that it led to a good outcome, and the CEO learned something from his boss that would help him to make better judgment calls going forward.

As the preceding stories illustrate, we view offering advice as a perfectly legitimate arrow to have in your coaching quiver. In fact, it is actually an essential one to have at your disposal.

The Best Advice

One of us has been a guest a couple of times on Rick Morris's radio program, "The Work-Life Balance," which is broadcast to more than 140 countries worldwide over VoiceAmerica Business Internet Talk Radio. Rick always wraps up the program by asking this question: "What's the best piece of advice you've ever gotten?"

The first time our coauthor was a guest on the program, he didn't know this question was coming. After reflecting for just a few seconds, he shared a really good piece of advice that someone close to him had offered – roughly thirty years earlier! That he had to reach so far back to come up with a great piece of advice seemed somehow significant. As he thought about this, he realized that he actually doesn't get much advice – even from people he respects tremendously and whose advice he would value.

The second time our coauthor joined Morris on his program, he knew the question was coming, and he shared a much more recent piece of advice from a colleague. Yet, the fact that he had so little to choose from in the way of advice from others still seemed telling.

Most people have probably been on the receiving end of advice they really did not find all that helpful. Perhaps it was because they did not see the source of the advice as credible. Or perhaps the advice was not delivered very effectively. Or maybe the timing was just bad.

However, we think it's noteworthy that the host of a weekly business radio program broadcast around the world ends every single program by asking about the best piece of advice his guest has ever gotten. Not the best *question* the guest has ever been asked. Not the time somebody drew a great solution out of his guest. But the best *advice* received. And we also think it's noteworthy that a professional who spends his life immersed in developmental activities struggled to come up with a response when asked that question.

Maybe, just maybe, the pendulum has swung too far away from giving advice and too far in the direction of asking good questions and listening, at least in the professional context. Food for thought, at least?

Providing Vision

One of us has recently been involved in some leader- and team-development work with a senior vice president (SVP) and his leadership team. As a part of the work, our coauthor facilitated dialogue among team members about what was going well and what could be going better within the team. For this dialogue, our coauthor used the popular "Stages of Team Development" model developed years ago by social psychologist Bruce Tuckman[39] (with a slight twist on the model that we discuss in Chapter 13).

The SVP had responsibility for all operations in the western region of the United States and reported up to corporate management in New York City. One of his challenges was that he actually got relatively little direction or even support from management above him, yet he was expected to provide direction for his organization that was in alignment with corporate management's expectations. This, of course, led to a situation in which his team felt that they needed a clearer sense of the "vision" for their part of the company, and they were looking to their SVP to take the lead in clarifying it.

Now, establishing a vision for an entire organization is a sufficiently large undertaking that effective leaders will no doubt enlist the help of at least some of their team members and employ a range of approaches to accomplish this outcome. Having said that, in this example the SVP's team was clearly and appropriately looking for him to take the lead on at least one key part of this: Clearly *explaining* to the team the realistic constraints and challenges they were facing by virtue of their relationship with corporate management. They also expected to learn the SVP's point of view on a realistic and compelling vision for the organization in light of those constraints and challenges.

---

[39] Tuckman, "Developmental Sequence in Small Groups."

So, while this SVP was rightly concerned about being too directive and was very keen to appropriately involve his team members, he acknowledged it was his responsibility to be the source of some much-needed clarity regarding the vision for the team. In other words, he realized that he was uniquely well-positioned to be able to *Explain* certain aspects of the vision and he committed to doing so, while remaining sensitive to the possibility of micromanagement with regards to the team's direction (or anything else, for that matter). After a number of sessions dealing with all of this, it was clear the team was successfully "re-forming" (to use Tuckman's language) and incrementally moving up through the stages of team development toward higher performance.

Stating Expectations

We mentioned in Chapter 3 that one of the top drivers of overall coaching effectiveness was: *"Sets clear performance expectations."* In other words, clearly stating expectations is one key coaching behavior, and it's another type of *Explain* coaching.

As Best Coach Michelle DiTondo puts it: "When something is complex and new to a person, and they haven't done the task, I try to be very clear with examples and expectations so that I'm not setting them up to fail." For instance, if she is working with a direct report on a complex organization redesign, she is pretty prescriptive about how to communicate to the employees who will be affected, and she will review the person's work product and give feedback on it. Keep in mind, here, that the people she is coaching at her level are themselves heads of Human Resources for large properties or leaders of corporate HR functions.

We can further illustrate this form of Explain conversation with a recent example from our own experience. Tom was the head of business development for a large organization which became a highly successful publicly traded company. One of us was serving as Tom's executive coach when he was given the task of running a couple of divisions as a divisional president. Tom was a very accomplished senior-level guy.

The company was preparing for a company-wide Town Hall meeting and Tom was in charge. He enlisted the help of his senior management team for various aspects of this event, and he asked one of his superstars – a sharp, talented guy named Robert – to cover a certain area. Robert responded apprehensively, saying that wasn't really a topic he knew much about.

The topic was actually something Robert knew very well, but he apparently didn't initially understand what he was being asked to cover. Tom recognized that Robert required a fuller explanation in order to understand the task in front of him. Once Tom took the opportunity to simply and briefly reword the task, Robert realized he could cover that topic and went about it with confidence.

We use this example of Tom and Robert because Robert is not a person who got hired to do menial tasks. He had a lot of experience and was very good at his job. What this story illustrates is that sometimes even relatively senior people who haven't done a specific task before, or haven't dealt with a specific circumstance or issue, can benefit from an Explain Coaching Conversation. And the skilled coach can handle the dialogue in a way that honors the dignity of both parties.

In trying to coach every person as a whole person, which we believe coaching should involve, the goal is to help improve their skills and motivation in as many areas as possible. That is when you can start empowering them (the subject of Chapter 10). Each coachee brings different skills and levels of motivation, and the coach address those skills and motivations on an individual level.

As a coach you might empower a person in one area but still need to explain other areas; this is the importance of holistic and adaptive coaching. Although we speak of moving people through the coaching conversations, coaching is not always about moving in a linear way through these techniques. They do not have to be applied across the board in each and every situation. This is what Tom was doing with Robert; he didn't need to micromanage him in other areas of his work, and Tom was primarily hands-off. But in the specific instance of taking charge of the Town Hall meeting, he needed to start with an explanation. After all, it's impossible to measure achievement if neither party outlines what an individual is expected to do.

Sharing Experience (or Expertise)

Sharing experience or expertise is something coaches can do to maximize people's performance and/or to help them develop their potential. Sometimes, expertise is technical in nature. For example, earlier on, we cited the example of a coach who understands how to do a DCF (Discounted Cash Flow analysis), and the coachee who would greatly appreciate and benefit from some Explain coaching in order to build understanding and skill in that area.

Sometimes, however, the knowledge passed along from coach to coachee is nontechnical in nature. This is the type of knowledge that Garry Ridge stresses as the senior tribal leader (or, in our terminology, head coach) at WD-40, and examples of this type of knowledge include folklore, myths, tales, practices, and that sort of thing.

To illustrate this type of coaching conversation, let us turn to Best Coach Matt Cole, an SVP of Cubic Corporation and President of Cubic Transportation Systems. When we asked Matt for examples of the types of coaching conversations he has with his people, he said, "Maybe it's a trait of mine, or maybe it's because I've been here fifteen years, but I have good instincts about what's going to happen." He went on to explain that he knows the clients, he knows the employees, he can run scenarios in his head, and he often has a sense as to what's most likely to happen.

"If I see a team on the wrong path," he explained, "I will say to them, 'Let me tell you what I think is going to happen unless we make some changes, and what the other party's response is going to be,' and so on." He said he will then walk them through the scenario and, essentially, tell them, "Here's what I want you to change, and here's why it will be better for the business." He went on to stress, "That's a form of coaching." And we agree: sharing your expertise or experience is indeed a form of coaching!

Here's another example of sharing experience as a form of Explain coaching. As management consultants, we travel . . . *a lot.* As the old joke goes, "What's the definition of a consultant?" Answer: "Someone who lives more than a thousand miles away."

At any rate, years ago at a previous firm, a couple of the coauthors were in a quarterly meeting at which most of the firm's two dozen or so employees were present. The meeting included everyone from relatively new Associates to tenured Managing Directors. Somehow, the conversation turned to the challenges associated with frequent business travel, and some of the newer people were expressing disillusionment with certain aspects of the road-warrior lifestyle, such as time away from family, frequent jet lag, and uncomfortable flights.

At one point, one of us – who by this point in his career had been traveling extensively for several years – spoke up and tried to explain a few things to his newer, less road-tested colleagues. "I hear you, and I sympathize with you" was the essence of his message. But, he continued, "I have to tell you that there are going to be times when you are stuck in a middle seat in coach on a flight from California to Hong Kong, and then you are going to have a bad night's sleep, and then you are going to have to get up the next morning and still be excellent in front of the client; that's just the nature of what we do."

Now, some of you reading this might be thinking, "Wow, what a jerk," or "Hmm, I'm not sure I'd want him to be teaching my employees about emotional intelligence." Fair enough. But, during the next break, one of the new Associates caught up with our coauthor and said, "Hey, I just want to thank you for what you said a while ago about the whole travel thing; that was a good reality check and just what I think we needed to hear."

The point is, sometimes effective coaching will feel quite warm and fuzzy – and sometimes it won't. In this situation, a "tribal leader" decided to offer some coaching to a few more junior tribal members. After sizing up the coaching context, he decided to candidly share, from his own perspective and experience, what it's really like to be a part of the road-warrior culture. And at least one of his coachees apparently thought it was appropriate and effective.

Giving Direction

Sometimes, the best thing a coach can do for a coachee is simply describe exactly how to do something. Here's a simple, personal example to illustrate. As a master's student, one of us took a quantitative methods class. In order to survive the class and learn the procedures necessary to conduct his own quantitative analysis, he used the instructor's in-class examples as a blueprint for how to replicate similar equations. By having the steps laid out clearly, he was able to emulate the same processes and conclusions to complete his own work.

As a group, great coaches do not shy away from just telling people what they need to know and do in order to achieve a given a task! For example, one of our Best Coaches, Darryl Albertson, was the CHRO of a global corporation at the time we interviewed him. Darryl gave the example of when he had hired a new head of Human Resources for the Asia Pacific region – someone who was going to be based in Sydney, Australia, a long way from the company's corporate headquarters (and the office of the coach we interviewed) in San Diego, California.

Darryl noted that the recent hire was new not only to certain countries she would serve but to the industry as well. Because of this, Darryl met with the new HR head frequently. Further, he used lots of checklists and other methods to ensure that the new HR leader was getting direction on specifics such as how to use the company's technology, who her key contacts would be, and so on. "In this case," Darryl told us, "she wanted me to tell her how to do things in her new company, so this approach worked extremely well."

Two things are noteworthy about this example. First, although this person was a relatively senior hire, she was still eager to get very clear direction from her new manager. This underscores the idea that leaders at all levels may benefit from an Explain approach at times. In other words, use of this approach does not have anything to do with one's seniority; it's all about what the Coaching Context calls for.

Second, this example involves two individuals who were not only in different offices, they were on different continents! As leadership development consultants, we often get asked some variation of the question: How does all of this apply in a remote working relationship? Our view is that it is possible to have every one of our five types of Coaching Conversations regardless of how the parties in the conversations are interacting: in person, by phone, via videoconference, or even by e-mail or text messaging.

We acknowledge, of course, that certain modes of expression are not available to the parties when they are communicating via phone or email or text messaging. For example, if a coachee is feeling discouraged, it may be harder to pick up on that via email, where you don't have access to body language and tone of voice. In many cases, however, an email or a text message is an effective coaching tool. For example, an email saying, "Paul is a key contact of yours, so you should schedule a meeting with him" is every bit as effective as conveying that message in person (and it's a lot less expensive, especially if one of you is in San Diego and the other is in Sydney).

Giving Feedback

One of the most important things a coach in almost any context does is provide feedback to the coachee. Indeed, research indicates that valid and well-delivered feedback – both positive and developmental – can have a significant positive impact on people's performance.[40] Feedback works best when it is specific and tied to a particular task, behavior, or goal. For example, telling employees they are doing well because they exceeded their goal by a specific percentage is more effective than simply saying "You're doing a good job." This

---

[40] Zheng, Diaz, Jing, and Chiaburu, "Positive and Negative Supervisor Developmental Feedback."

level of specificity provides coachees with the details they need to keep or begin doing what they need to do to be successful, or gives them a framework for understanding what's not working and the impact it has on the team or organization.

An approach to delivering feedback that we like, personally use, and often teach to the leaders we work with is the Situation, Behavior, Impact (or SBI) model developed by the Center for Creative Leadership.[41] This is largely a coach-directed interaction that involves three steps. First, you explain to the coachee a situation in which you observed some behavior that you would like to provide feedback on. Second, you describe the behavior in a succinct, fact-based, nonjudgmental way. Finally, you explain what you believe the impact of the behavior to be.

One of the things we like about this approach is that it can be used to deliver both positive and developmental feedback (sometimes referred to as "constructive criticism"). For example, a coach might say to a coachee right after a meeting, "Hey, when the CEO posed that tough question to you (Situation), I noticed that you had an immediate, well-supported, and articulate response (Behavior), and I suspect that exchange boosted your credibility a lot with the whole executive team (Impact)." This type of statement is, of course, different from "praise" along the lines of "nice job" in that it is very specific. Indeed, this example reflects the idea that positive feedback should adhere to the same guidelines as developmental feedback (in terms of specificity, immediacy, etc.).

The question is, why is it important for coaches to deliver both positive *and* developmental feedback? An article by Jack Zenger

---

[41] Weitzel, Feedback That Works.

and Joseph Folkman, "The Ideal Praise-to-Criticism Ratio," notes that only positive feedback can "motivate people to continue to do what they're already doing well, with more vigor, determination and creativity." Negative or developmental feedback, on the other hand, is important because it "serves as a guard against complacency and groupthink"by acting like a "whack on the side of the head"that has the ability to really grab one's attention.

Although the research varies, experts generally agree that providing more positive than developmental feedback works best. For example, Marcial Losada and Emily Heaphy[42] found a ratio of three positive statements for every negative or developmental one to be optimal, while another study found the ideal ration to be five-to-one, but still skewed in the direction of more positive than developmental feedback.[43]

So, while coaches may want to err on the side of more positive feedback, it's clearly a coach's job to provide developmental feedback, too, and the SBI approach can work just as well with that type of feedback. You might say to a coachee, "I noticed that during that meeting (Situation), you appeared to be looking at your phone quite a bit (Behavior), and it might have given the other people in the meeting the impression that you were not fully engaged in the discussion (Impact)." It is important to note that the "behavior" statement in this example is intended to be as objective as possible. In other words, rather than saying, "You were checking messages throughout the meeting,"you stick with what you actually observed ("you appeared to be looking at your phone"). We believe that by

---

[42] Losada and Heaphy, "Positivity and Connectivity in the Performance of Business Teams."
[43] Gottman, *The Seven Principles for Making Marriage Work.*

avoiding more judgmental language, you minimize the likelihood that the coachee will immediately go on the defensive.

In fact, especially when using the SBI model to provide developmental feedback, we think it's important to add another step: *Ask* the coachee a question to get his or her perspective on the feedback just provided. Therefore, when we use this model, we refer to it as SBIA.

The "ask" in this approach may be an actual question, such as, "What's your take on what I've just said?" Or, it may be what we call a prompt, such as, "Help me understand your point of view on this." In either case, the objective is to share the feedback as succinctly and objectively as possible, and then to put the ball in the coachee's court in order to try to understand the situation from his or her perspective.

Best Coach Matt Cole gave us a great example of the use of the SBIA model in a real-life situation. He had a direct report, the CFO of the company – we'll call him Herb – who was struggling in a few areas. After having gotten feedback on this problem from a number of members of his executive team, feedback that reinforced Matt's concerns about Herb, he sat down to talk with him.

Matt said that in order to help Herb understand the feedback, he was quite direct with him. When we asked Matt exactly how he did that, he said, "I told him, 'When you did X, Y, and Z, here's how you made me feel.'" When pressed for an example, Matt said in one instance he used this basic approach when he was trying to stand up a start-up company, and Herb was reluctant to provide funding because he disagreed with the idea. This not only nicely demonstrates use of the SBI approach in an actual business conversation (minus the "A" for "ask" in this case), it also illustrates how this approach can be used for everything from small disagreements to more significant issues involving capital investments.

There are a few other things we find interesting about this example. First, Matt noted that before getting into the feedback, he really stressed to Herb that he was trying to do the right thing for *him*. In our experience, leaders often shy away from providing tough feedback to their employees for fear of offending them, creating conflict, hurting the relationship, and so on. And these are all valid concerns.

But, consistent with the research cited by Kerry Patterson and his coauthors in the book *Crucial Conversations*,[44] if you are delivering a potentially challenging message and start by reassuring the person on the receiving end that you have his or her best interests at heart, it can go a long way toward making the conversation a constructive one. And that's exactly what Matt did with Herb.

Another thing that's interesting about this example is that Matt noted that, in addition to his efforts to personally coach Herb in areas where he was struggling, he also hired a professional executive coach for Herb, and that coach worked with him for several months. So, Herb was getting feedback and coaching from different sources. We have seen plenty of cases over the years of managers hiring professional coaches as essentially surrogates – meaning that the coaches are doing what the managers themselves should be doing. And we are not fans of the "coach as surrogate" approach. But in this case, Matt took it upon himself to ensure that the employee was getting ample coaching – *both* from himself *and* from someone who could bring an outside perspective and deep coaching skills to the situation.

---

[44] Patterson, Grenny, McMillan, and Switzler, *Crucial Conversations*.

Finally, we don't know if Matt had actually been taught some version of the SBIA model at some point or whether he just naturally used a variation, sensing that it would be an effective way to handle this thorny matter. But we will say that we often teach this model to managers in our leadership development workshops, and we have found it to be a great, practical tool for having a particular type of Explain Coaching Conversation – one where the coach needs to deliver some feedback to a coachee.

As a postscript: Matt reported that because of all the coaching Herb received, "I'm delighted with where he's at now – he is thriving, and he collaborates really well." Matt then noted that he could have just given up on Herb, but he truly believed that by personally coaching him, and also arranging for Herb to work with a professional coach, he could save a very valued member of his team. And he was right!

Explain in Action

Of course, this idea that people sometimes need things explained to them, and that sometimes coaches need a method for effectively doing so, is far from revolutionary. Indeed, organizations sometimes develop their own models and approaches for just such a purpose. For example, the Boy Scouts of America utilizes the "EDGE" method[45] when teaching someone a new skill. EDGE stands for:

- Explain how it's done
- Demonstrate the steps
- Guide learners as they practice
- Enable them to succeed on their own

The primary point here is that Explain conversations are widely considered to be a legitimate way of helping people perform well in countless different contexts, and this has been the case since

---

[45] *Scouts BSA. First Edition 1911.*

the dawn of time. So, our goal with this chapter is not to argue that this is a common and legitimate form of communication; we believe that's self-evident. Rather, our goal is to position this type of communication squarely within the realm of effective coaching so that coaches and would-be coaches are not avoiding this approach to influencing people for fear of being or seeming more directive than a coach should be.

When to Have an Explain Conversation

As is the case with every type of coaching conversation, there is a judgment element in determining whether the Coaching Context warrants use of an Explain coaching approach. And as with any adaptable coaching or teaching approach, the form of explanation needs to be adjusted based on each individual and his or her specific needs.

Put simply, you should initiate an Explain Coaching Conversation when the Coaching Cue of "inexperience" is present (or, to put it differently, when the coachee's Central Issue is lack of or need for better understanding of how to perform in some area). As Best Coach Kevin Freiberg, best-selling author and very experienced and accomplished keynote speaker, put it: "I think you need to Explain when the coachee's competence is low," and he elaborated by saying, "you need to help build up skill before you do anything else."

Kevin then offered an example from personal experience. He said that if he were coaching someone who was relatively inexperienced at giving presentations in front of large groups, and was therefore very nervous before doing so on a particular occasion, he would lean toward having an Explain conversation: "Asking a bunch of questions would be inefficient for the other person, and inefficient for you as the coach."

More specifically, Kevin indicated that he would be inclined to explain a technique that might be helpful to the coachee, such as a bit of advice on how to read an audience, which would probably help the presenter get comfortable speaking much more quickly than more of a dialogic approach. The key is to try to help coachees have what Kevin calls a "small win," knowing that multiple small wins is a way of keeping coachees engaged in the coaching process as they grow and develop.

In other words, sometimes what the coachee needs, first and foremost, is the ability to do the job at hand. It was noted earlier that one aspect of the coaching context is the competence of the coachee. And we believe that when a coachee's competence is relatively low, then building ability in the area in which he or she is receiving coaching should be the coach's priority.

The reason we believe this is that, as we have long expressed to the leaders we work with, "skill drives will." In other words, if you are trying to coach someone who, relatively speaking, lacks both skill (or competence) and will (or commitment) in a given area, by focusing on building the coachee's *skill* or *competence* in the area at hand, there is a good chance that his or her *will* or *commitment* will improve as a result.

Sometimes, however, a coachee has sufficient skill or competence to be able to contribute in a meaningful way to some approach to a given issue, even if he or she is not yet at a point where a coach can simply cut the coachee loose. In this sort of situation, we believe the Explore Coaching Conversation is appropriate, and that is the subject of the next chapter.

The EXPLORE Coaching Conversation

chapter 8

"Every problem contains within itself the seeds of its own solution."

~ NORMAN VINCENT PEALE – Author and pioneer in the area of positive thinking

INTERESTINGLY, while both our research and our experience suggest that there are numerous types of *Explain* Coaching Conversation, (which you just read about in the last chapter), we believe that almost any *Explore* Coaching Conversation essentially seeks to accomplish one thing: To help a coachee identify options for how to address some sort of issue, and then to help the coachee settle on one or more options to actually follow through on.

The key for this type of conversation, of course, is that the coach should be relying as much as possible on asking good questions to guide the conversation rather than falling prey to the natural tendency many people have to want to start giving advice. Again, giving advice is a perfectly valid coaching approach, and we believe coaches should be completely comfortable using it when the context warrants it. But this chapter is devoted to what might be thought of as the "question-asking" rather than the "statement-making" approach to coaching.

We found support for the Explore type of Coaching Conversation in the statistical analysis we conducted as a part of the research for this book. Specifically, one of the top drivers or predictors of overall coaching effectiveness, based on that analysis, was the 360-degree feedback item, *"Encourages cooperative problem-solving."* We think that coaching behavior captures the essence of the Explore conversation. In other words, unlike the Explain conversation, in which the coach is quite directive, or the Empower conversation, in which the coachee is essentially in the driver's seat, the Explore conversation involves collaboration and brainstorming between coach and coachee.

Now, we noted earlier that there are numerous existing models that explain (ironically) how to have a "question-asking" type of coaching conversation. Two specific examples we cited were the GROW model developed by Alan Fine and others, and the FUEL model developed by John Zenger and Kathleen Stinnett. Avion Consulting has developed our own version of a model for an Explore conversation, which is as follows.

Explore and the ISEE Model

While we would not want to offer another model for how to structure a question-asking approach to coaching just for the sake of offering another model, we do have our own point of view regarding what effective "question-asking"– or Explore Coaching — involves. And we, too, have broken this sort of conversation down into four key steps (see Figure 8.1): Issue, Situation, Exploration, and Execution. To illustrate what such a conversation might look and sound like, we will provide a running example throughout the explanation of our model, and then offer a couple more examples afterward.

Figure 8.1 | *ISEE Model*

We'd like to begin this discussion by referring once again to an earlier book by Avion Consulting, *How Leaders Improve*.[46] As we argued earlier, while that book and the research on which it is based deal with how leaders in particular improve, we believe the insights it offers serve as a good playbook for anybody who seeks to become more effective in a given area – whether that person is in a leadership role or not.

We want to re-visit one insight from that book that we touched on earlier, the idea that those who improve the most often begin with what we call a Central Issue. This is a single word or short phrase that represents the key area in which someone seeks to become more effective, which then brings focus to any improvement effort

---
[46] Gates, Graddy, and Lindekens, *How Leaders Improve*.

and makes the key area for improvement memorable. And that idea serves as the starting place for our four-step approach to having an Explore Coaching Conversation.

Issue

The first thing that we believe a good coach will do when having an Explore Coaching Conversation is to help the coachee isolate the *issue* he or she wishes to address. This could be a problem that needs to be addressed, a risk that needs to be mitigated, or an opportunity that the coachee wants to take advantage of.

And we think the coach can help the coachee get clarity on the issue by asking these key questions. The first, quite simply, is: "What is it you want to accomplish?" And the second is: "What would a good outcome be?"

For example, Mike Twyman, one of our Best Coaches and the division President of a defense contracting organization, noted that in his industry, if a company has the best technical solution at the lowest price, that company usually wins the contract. And since, as he put it, "most teams can always come up with a better widget," he tends to ask lots of hard questions regarding the price target his company needs to be at for a given bid, and why. To put it in the terminology of our ISEE model, the issue in this example is figuring out how this leader's team can come up with a bid that is priced in such a way that his company wins the contract.

Situation

Having helped the coachee isolate the issue to be addressed in the coaching conversation (or conversations, if the issue is too significant and/or complicated to be addressed in a single interaction), the next step is for the coach to help the coachee explore the *situation,* with a focus on possible causes of whatever the issue is. There are several relatively simple but excellent questions to pose during this step in an Explore conversation, questions such as:

- What should I understand about the context?
- What's causing the issue?
- What has kept the issue from being addressed so far?

Or, if it's more of an opportunity rather than a problem or risk, a good question might be: What has kept you from taking advantage of this opportunity so far?

Beyond these questions, which are pretty straightforward, we think there are two other important but less frequently used questions for an Explore Coaching Conversation. The first is, "What are *you* contributing to this situation?" Humans have a tendency to want to attribute their issues to other people or factors outside of their control, but we think it's helpful and appropriate to get coachees to reflect on how their perspective and/or behavior may be a factor.

But, in fairness, it's also important to ask the second, follow-up question: "What do you think *other* contributing factors might be?" This could include organizational policies, resource constraints, colleagues with their own agendas, and countless other factors.

To stick with our defense contractor example, the leader may ask questions of his team members along the lines of, "What's causing our pricing to be where it currently is? What's causing our cost-structure for this bid to be what it is?" And so on. A leader may have his or her own point of view as to how to answer these questions, but our Best Coach in this example, Mike, said he tends to lead primarily by asking good questions in a situation like this, rather than leading with his own point of view. And this makes sense; why have a talented team of professionals working on a bid if you are not going to tap into their knowledge and expertise by asking good questions?

Exploration

Next, the coach should *explore* options for addressing the causes of the problem, and thus – hopefully – dealing effectively with whatever the issue is. And here's where we agree completely with all the coaching models out there that encourage the coach to try to draw solutions out of the coachee. We believe this part of the Explore Coaching Conversation should be thought of as a two-person brainstorming session, where the coach begins the brainstorming part of the conversation by asking some variation of the question, "In light of the situation we've just discussed, what options can you can think of for addressing the issue?"

And then we encourage the coach to ask the magic question: "What else?" An analogy we like to use is that of a glass of water, in which the coachee's ideas for addressing the issue are the water. The idea is to *allow the coachee to completely empty his or her water glass.* Then, and only then, might you as the coach want to offer your own suggestions.

Returning to our defense contractor example, the obvious next step in using the Explore approach would be for our leader, Mike, to ask the team what options they can think of for reducing the cost structure in order to lower the pricing in a bid. Such questions might include, among others:

- What are the assumptions behind our current pricing?
- What assumptions might be questionable?

- What are some creative options for providing the same or comparable features at a reduced cost?

- What features might we be able to remove from our bid without fundamentally sacrificing the functionality or quality of what we need to deliver to the client?

Execution

Finally, in an Explore conversation you help the coachee decide what he or she is going to actually execute, and how. In other words, this step involves a decision as to exactly what the coachee is going to do to address whatever the issue is, and how he or she is going to follow through on that decision. We think this involves asking the question, "In light of everything we've discussed, what do you plan to do?" And then, "What are your next steps?" We believe it's important, whenever possible, for the coachee to leave the coaching conversation with at least a good idea of what to do almost immediately in order to follow up on whatever the two of you have discussed.

Getting back to our running example one last time, it's obviously important to wrap up an Explore Coaching Conversation regarding pricing for a bid by deciding what the plan is in order to come in at the most competitive possible price point. So, consistent with the sample questions above, here is the opportunity for our leader, Mike, to ask his coachee or even the entire team, "Of the options we have discussed, which ones do we want to adopt? And what are our next steps?" Again, the leader may have a clear sense of how to proceed, but if the team is made up of strong players – as was the case with this example – it only makes sense to at least initially get the other person's or even the entire team's take on the best way to proceed.

ISEE in Action

We think it's helpful to share a couple of additional real-life examples to illustrate what the ISEE approach looks like in an actual interaction. And, as with any model, there is both the "letter of the law" (following a model step-by-step) and the "spirit of the law" (adhering to at least the essence of a model or an approach). At a minimum, we believe these examples should give you a good sense of the essence of our model.

Figure 8.1 | *ISEE Model*

When we talked with Best Coach Matt Cole about why he is so highly regarded as a coach, he gave us an example of a recent coaching conversation that we think illustrates a few important points.

Matt explained that he had had a conversation with a direct report literally the day before we talked with him about his approach to coaching. It concerned an issue another team had presented to him and his team. And, as Matt put it, "My direct report was complimenting me on coaching the team to the right answer, and I had not thought about it that way; I was just trying to ask them questions to help them get to an answer, because they were more educated on it than I was."

From Matt's perspective, he was just trying to help some direct reports address an issue. But the feedback he got from one of those direct reports was that he was essentially teaching them to solve the problem.

One point of this brief story is that one context in which to have an Explore Coaching Conversation is, quite simply, when you are trying to help one or more people address an issue, and when the people being coached actually have more subject matter expertise on the issue at hand than you do. This brings up once again our notion of credibility as an aspect of the Coaching Context. In this example, Matt may not have had as much "content expertise" as his direct reports, but he had substantial "process skill," meaning that he knew how to effectively coach others just by asking good questions.

A second point this story illustrates is that any coaching conversation (in this case, Explore) may be a deliberate one initiated by a coach – or it may not be. In this case, Matt himself didn't even really consider it to be a coaching conversation until after the fact, when a direct report pointed out that Matt had done a great job of "coaching the team to the answer."

Finally, we think this story gets at the idea, discussed earlier, that effective coaching generally serves more than one key purpose. First, if it's good coaching, the conversation should result in some increase in performance or resolution of some issue. And second, it should develop the person or people being coached such that they are more competent, confident, and committed as a result – and thus better able to achieve the positive outcome on their own in the future.

Best Coach Dr. Mark Brouker gave us another example to illustrate what an effective Explore Coaching Conversation looks like. When Mark moved into the COO role for ten naval hospitals, there were well over fifty Key Performance Indicators (KPIs) for this hospital system. Mark and the Admiral to whom he reported agreed that this was way too many KPIs to track, so they determined to find a way to streamline them.

The problem was that the team that had created these KPIs had worked very hard to do so, and that same team did, in Mark's words, a "tremendous job" of tracking them. It was essentially their baby. So, simply "blowing up" this measurement system would have been extremely demotivating for the members of that team, and for the leader in particular.

So, Mark started making it a point during meetings with that team leader to ask good questions about the process. For example, he would ask, "How long does it take your team to put together these fifty or so KPIs?" Or, "How might we be able to simplify this?" Then later, "What might the advantages of reducing the number of KPIs be?" After a few meetings exploring the situation together in this manner, the team leader ultimately suggested that they reduce the number of KPIs to sixteen – which they did.

Mark, of course, had realized early on that such streamlining would be a good move. But by exploring the matter with the person who owned the process, they got to a good outcome, and the team leader was undoubtedly more engaged and bought into the decision as a result. If Mark had simply explained what he wanted done, the team leader would surely have complied – but at what cost?

In sum, when we interviewed our Best Coaches, they shared a couple of important insights about this type of coaching. First, exploring is a way to align a person's expectations with the reality of a situation where, for example, they want to achieve some career goal but do not understand what skills and experiences it really takes to be successful in a bigger or different role. And second, an Explore conversation is especially appropriate when it is best for a coachee to form his or her own conclusions and next steps, so the individual both learns and is more committed to the required development path.

Case Study

A recent coaching conversation one of us had with a leader he is working with illustrates both the context in which an Explore Coaching Conversation is appropriate, as well as the way in which such a conversation might realistically unfold. The coachee in this example – we'll call her Sophia – is a relatively senior leader in one of the coach's client organizations. And Sophia is, as of this writing, participating in one of our firm's high-potential leadership development programs.

By the time the conversation in this case study took place, our coauthor had been coaching Sophia for several months and felt like he was starting to understand reasonably well what made her tick **as** a leader: Her strengths, her areas for development, and so on. And our coauthor coach was thinking hard about how to communicate with Sophia in such a way that she might have some sort of breakthrough in dealing with a challenging situation at work.

The challenging situation involved Sophia's manager, whom the coach also knows. So, when Sophia described her manager as smart, well-educated, and accomplished – yet someone who had a hard time reading situations and other people and adapting accordingly – her description resonated with our coauthor.

Sophia's manager had come to Sophia for guidance on how to handle working with certain colleagues, including her own boss. The manager perceived Sophia to be strong in the areas where she herself struggled. And this, too, rang true with our coauthor, who had seen firsthand the coachee's strengths in areas that, collectively, could be thought of as "emotional intelligence."

The problem, according to Sophia, was that her manager tended to ask for guidance from others and then not really act on it. In the situation at hand, the manager's struggles were starting to affect one whole part of the organization — including Sophia and her team. So, Sophia asked for some time to talk with our coauthor about the matter.

Now, let's pause and consider the various aspects of the Coaching Context here. As discussed in Chapter 5, the first aspect of the Coaching Context is the Credibility of the Coach. In this example, we believe the evidence suggests that Sophia perceived our coauthor as credible. Their coaching conversations were voluntary, meaning that Sophia only reached out to our coauthor when she thought the conversation might be helpful. Also, at several points in the conversation (and in previous coaching conversations), Sophia specifically asked for her coach's advice. All of this suggests that our coauthor had credibility in Sophia's mind.

The second aspect of the Coaching Context is the Criticality of the Issue. As noted above, the goal of helping her manager improve in the area in which she was struggling had indeed become critical for Sophia, as her manager's struggles were now having a negative impact on the organization, including Sophia's team.

The next few aspects of the Coaching Context have to do with the coachee – Confidence, Competence, and Commitment. In this example, Sophia was clearly committed to trying to address the issue; after all, she had proactively reached out for some coaching precisely because she was committed to being helpful to her manager, thus helping both her own team and the broader organization, as well.

Sophia's competence and confidence, on the other hand, were at least a little shaky. The evidence for this was that she had tried on a few occasions to help her manager to address her challenges, including in the conversation where the manager specifically asked for her help, and so far, nothing seemed to be working. At the same time, Sophia clearly seemed to be more competent and confident than her manager in the very area in which the manager was seeking counsel – reading people and situations and adapting accordingly.

Now, it would be really nice if we could simply plug all this data into a formula and have it spit out the "right" coaching approach. However, we believe the real world is not so neat and tidy. As discussed earlier, deciding on the best approach requires *judgment* on the part of the coach.

Mentally evaluating the best coaching option in this situation, our coauthor quickly eliminated the Encourage, Empower, and Elevate Coaching Conversations. After all, Sophia herself had chosen to take forty-five minutes out of her busy schedule specifically to ask, "I was just wondering if you have any advice on how to handle this challenging situation?"

Early in the conversation, our coauthor could just have launched into Explain mode. It would have been easy to give Sophia the advice she had specifically requested. But the coach realized that he was not entirely clear on the Central Issue she sought to address.

So, he went into Explore mode. More specifically, he asked a few questions, in part to better understand what the Central Issue was, but more so to get *Sophia* thinking about the Central Issue she was trying to address. Sophia outlined a few different issues she was concerned about, and our coauthor repeated them back to her in his own words. He then asked, "Which of these is your biggest priority?" This helped Sophia focus on *the* issue she most wanted to discuss, at least in this coaching conversation. And that Central Issue was this: To help her manager be more adaptable, particularly when dealing with her own boss.

Having used the Explore approach to help Sophia identify the Central Issue for the coaching conversation, our coauthor then reminded Sophia that she had said her manager had a tendency to solicit advice yet did not put whatever advice she received into practice. Our coauthor continued in Explore mode by asking the question, "Why do you think that is?" He had a hypothesis about this but wanted Sophia to think about this before he expressed his point of view.

Sophia offered a few thoughts about why her manager apparently had a pattern of asking for advice and not taking it. Then our coauthor offered up one more possibility, asking, "Do you think it might be because she is not coming up with the solutions on her own?" Sophia reacted as if a lightbulb had lit up in her mind. "You know, I think that's *exactly* what the problem is!"

At this point, our coauthor shifted from Explore to Explain and provided a little feedback, pointing out that in their coaching conversations to date, he had noticed that Sophia often referred to advice she had given to others. In fact, because she was perceived as someone with lots of emotional intelligence, people often sought her advice, particularly on "people issues." Yet, if the person soliciting the advice was not actually doing what she was advised to do, perhaps that was not the best approach.

They explored this a bit further, and Sophia concluded that she needed to go back and use more of a "question-asking" approach with her manager. And the questions she committed to asking had to do with two main things: First, trying to help her manager identify the Central Issue to work on; and second, trying to get her manager to come up with possible ways of addressing the issue on her own. This stemmed from the premise that she would probably come up with a good solution on her own and that she might well be more committed to the solution if she herself had come up with it. While the verdict is not yet in regarding Sophia's approach as of this writing, our coauthor is nonetheless confident that Sophia has a good plan.

Deconstructing the Case

Now, let's highlight a few lessons from this example. First, while we have not applied a simple formula to this situation in order to come up with the "right" approach, our coauthor's careful consideration of the Coaching Context allowed him to quickly eliminate a few different options for at least the majority of this conversation. And, once he determined that the conversation needed to be somewhere in the Explain-to-Explore range, he spent time toggling back and forth, so to speak, between those two types of conversations.

He emphasized helping the coachee explore such questions as what the Central Issue was, why previous efforts to help had not been successful, and what some other options might be going forward.

Second, this case illustrates that multiple approaches may be used by a coach during a given coaching session. While the primary approach used by the coach in this conversation was Explore, he also used some Explain (offering his own observations and thoughts), and even some Encourage (by stressing that he did, in fact, agree with the coachee's self-assessment that she had some strengths in areas that her manager struggled with).

Finally, this example actually represents two different Explore conversations, all in one story. One Explore conversation was between the coach (our coauthor sharing the story) and the coachee (the leader with whom he was having the coaching conversation). The other Explore conversation – which presumably took place later – was going to be between the coachee and her manager. In essence, the coachee was going to become the coach and was committing to use more of an Explore approach with her manager, instead of automatically gravitating toward her natural "advice-giving" style of coaching.

One last point. In Chapter 6, we discussed the idea of Coaching Cues that can serve as a sort of short-cut in order to help a coach quickly decide what the best approach to a given coaching conversation might be. To review, those cues were: Inexperienced (Explain), Uncertain (Explore), Hesitant (Encourage), Successful (Empower), and Accomplished (Elevate).

Now, ask yourself: Which of these cues was most clearly present in the example just described? The coachee was not *inexperienced* in the situation; indeed, she had reported to this manager for some time. She was not really *hesitant.* But neither was she especially *successful* or *accomplished* in this area, which was why she was asking for help from her leadership coach. Indeed, we think the best way to describe the coachee's frame of mind was that she was simply *uncertain* about how to proceed, in which case an Explore conversation would likely be the best approach. And, indeed, it seemed to be a good fit for this particular conversation.

Consistent with this example, an Explore Coaching Conversation is especially appropriate when someone needs to come to his or her own conclusions, and when you can have a dialogue so that the coachee can think through variables, options, and the best path forward. Several of our Best Coaches shared specific examples of times they explored a topic with someone but did not lead the individual to a specific outcome. Rather, by asking the right questions, our Best Coaches got their coachees to see things differently. As a result, they worked on their development in a different way, but ultimately by their own choice.

A Few Key Points About the Explore Conversation

Here are a few additional key points that are especially relevant to the Explore Coaching Conversation. First, an Explore conversation may actually be more of an ongoing dialogue that lasts over days, weeks, or even months. As Best Coach Elisabet Hearn, CEO of Katapult Partners, and author of *Leading Teams: 10 Challenges,10 Solutions* and *The Team Formula*, puts it, "This type of conversation can go deep and last coaching session after coaching session to allow for proper reflection and testing of ideas, perspectives, and so on." Even the term "explore" connotes a potentially circuitous route with some uncertainty, missteps, and perhaps even a bit of adventure along the way!

Second, it's important to allow the coachee during an Explore Coaching Conversation to arrive at his or her own solution to whatever the issue is, if at all possible. Best Coach Mary Watson, Executive Director at AccentCare, agrees. "It's important to explore with people but, in the end, have them come to their own conclusions. I use this when those I am coaching have encountered some kind of barrier and using dialogue will help access reasons why and different perspectives. It will also help gain their commitment to a solution."

Mary then recounted the story of a time she was coaching an HR professional who wanted to implement a bunch of new initiatives, including moving to a four-day workweek. Mary said she knew that would not fly in her particular organization, but she also realized that she had to "let [the coachee] down easy so as to not deflate his passion." Instead, her goal was to harness his passion and redirect it so that his creativity and drive might be better leveraged.

So, Mary and the coachee talked about the pros and cons of a four-day workweek, how it would be received, and how much employees' workload might increase during the four days they would be at work. While she acknowledges that she gave him some guidance and perspective, ultimately, after exploring the issue at some length, the coachee came to the conclusion that, while a good idea in concept, what he initially wanted to propose wouldn't work in the company culture. Furthermore, he understood the reasons why, and he very likely bought into the conclusion they arrived at much more than if Mary had used more of an Explain approach, essentially telling him it was a bad idea and he should not propose it.

Third, when you anticipate having an Explore conversation, it's helpful to prepare specific questions so that you are not always trying to come up with good ones on the spot. For example, Best Coach Hina Asad, Clinical Supervisor at AccentCare, explained to us that one of her favorite ways to get the coachee thinking and talking is to say, "Walk me through what you would do."

And, interestingly, this example illustrates something else about the Explore conversation, which is that sometimes the best coaching questions aren't actually questions at all; they are prompts, or statements that elicit some sort of response from the coachee. Either way, the goal of an Explore conversation is to get the coachee, rather than the coach, to do most of the problem-solving.

Fourth, the Explore Coaching Conversation is especially well-suited to what might be referred to as "coaching upward." Any of our Five Coaching Conversations might be appropriate when seeking to positively influence people at all different levels. However, given the power differential inherent in a relationship between a more senior person and a more junior person, asking good questions may be the best, or at least the safest, approach to coaching someone higher up in the organizational hierarchy.

Best Coach Ryan Fletcher, Risk and Information Services Manager at AMERISAFE, illustrated this with the following example. He and his then-boss had to be in alignment on an important legal issue, and his approach was to explore different ideas in order to get to a point where they were both on the same page. While some superior-subordinate relationships may be such that the more junior person can insist, "This is what we should do," a more effective approach in that context may well be to say, "Here's my perspective. What's yours?" In other words, *explore!*

When to Have the Explore Conversation

A good time to initiate an Explore Coaching Conversation is when the Coaching Cue of "uncertainty" is present and the coachee's Central Issue is lack of a plan and/or a need for a "breakthrough."

In other words, the Central Issue is that the coachee needs (or at least would greatly benefit from) some dialogue with someone who has some combination of content expertise and/or process skill – that is, a good coach. The key, of course, is that the coachee must at least have enough competence (or ability) to be able to engage in a dialogue about options for addressing some important matter, and to be the person in the coaching interaction to ultimately decide on the best way forward.

Of course, it is probably clear that the type of situation just described captures the default approach to coaching, at least as it is espoused by other coaching experts, coaching certification firms, and so on. And, indeed, we think it's often exactly the right approach. Frankly, sometimes what a coachee needs more than anything is just someone to serve as a sounding board and conversation facilitator. And we believe this is particularly the case when a coaching conversation deals with relatively non-technical issues.

Let us put all of this together with another real-life example. One of us was serving as the coach of a relatively senior leader in one of our client organizations a few years ago. This leader was very smart and accomplished, but got feedback that he was frequently over-extended, not good at follow-through, and generally just sort of inefficient.

While not every coaching conversation lends itself to the coach just asking good questions, listening, and helping the coachee come up with his or her own solution to some problem – this one certainly did. So, our coauthor entered into the conversation mindful that what the coachee needed, more than anything, was just some structured dialogue.

Our coauthor helped the coachee focus on one specific issue that seemed to be hindering his effectiveness — the fact that he was chronically way behind in his emails. He then helped the coachee essentially diagnose reasons for that problem, and then discuss options for addressing it. Our coauthor had a couple ideas of his own to share, but it was in the spirit of brainstorming rather than giving advice. Finally, he helped the coachee come up with a plan for moving forward.

During the next coaching conversation a few weeks later, the coachee proudly announced that he had gotten his email box down to zero, with old emails properly filed, and that he had implemented the system the two had discussed and managed to keep his inbox at a reasonable number of emails. And, more importantly, he was doing a much better job of responding to his colleagues' emails within a respectful amount of time, which was helping in terms of his credibility, his relationships with his co-workers, and ultimately the effectiveness of all involved.

Now, the coach in this example could have started making suggestions as soon as the problem to be addressed was clarified. However, this was not rocket science. In other words, this was not one of those times when the coach clearly had a form of *content expertise* that the coachee lacked. Rather, what the coachee most needed was simply some open dialogue with someone – presumably with a coach who had enough *process skill* to be able to facilitate the conversation in such a way that they arrived at a good outcome.

Moving Back and Forth

We decided to close this chapter with another story from Best Coach Matt Cole because it nicely captures the way a skillful coach can move back and forth between the Explain and Explore Coaching Conversations.

Matt recounted to us that he had a great guy running his North American business – we'll call him Ruben – but he was experiencing some challenges in his role. For example, there were some issues with the financial performance of the region Ruben was in charge of, and he seemed to be having a hard time discerning the cause of the problem. Matt was confident that Ruben had great value to offer, so, as the coach, Matt started with some evaluation. For about six months, he frequently visited the clients in Ruben's region and took other steps to get into the details of what and where the issues were. All of this allowed Matt to develop a deep understanding of the situation and the context. Then, Matt did a mid-year review with Ruben, using what we would call an Explain approach to provide some direct feedback about what he was seeing.

As is often the case, that Explain Coaching Conversation became more of an Explore conversation. In other words, once Matt felt certain that Ruben clearly understood the messages being communicated to him, they began exploring options to resolve the problem.

For example, together they explored alternative organizational structures, and once they had agreed at a high level on what a more effective structure might be, they worked together on the design of the new structure. Interestingly, the new structure involved Ruben taking on a smaller (though still very large) role as the West Coast Regional Manager. Ruben unreservedly bought into the solutions they ended up adopting because Matt had effectively used the Explain approach to help Ruben understand the nature and seriousness of the issue, and then brought the Explore approach into play in order to involve Ruben in coming up with the solution.

Fast-forward three years. Matt's division within the company has had a record year – and much of that has been because of Ruben's improved performance. As Matt put it, Ruben "had an exceptional year – I just gave him a great performance review, and customer relationships have improved dramatically."

One very important thing Matt stressed about this story is that it was a long journey, taking place over the course of about a year. But all that effort clearly was worth it. Ruben, according to Matt, "is happier, he's thriving in his job, and even his work-life balance has improved." And this is the beauty of effective coaching in the organizational realm.

The ENCOURAGE Coaching Conversation

chapter 9

"People will forget what you said, people will forget what you did, but people will never forget how you made them feel."

~ MAYA ANGELOU – Poet, singer, memoirist and civil rights activist

WHEN IT COMES TO REALIZING THE POTENTIAL AND MAXIMIZING THE PERFORMANCE OF A COACHEE, MOTIVATION IS AT LEAST HALF THE BATTLE.

In Chapter 5, we cited a distinguished thinker in the field of leadership, Dr. Steve Kerr, who argued that there are two key factors that drive performance: Ability and Motivation. In the prior two chapters we focused on coaching approaches that, to varying degrees, deal with the first part of Dr. Kerr's formula: A coachee's *ability* to perform in a given area. The Explain Coaching Conversation focuses on a coachee's ability or competence to perform well in a given area by providing clear direction, though that direction can take a number of different forms. And the Explore Coaching Conversation, while less directive than the Explain approach, is nevertheless centered on helping a coachee come up with a sound approach to addressing some sort of issue.

In this chapter we turn our attention to a third coaching approach, which we call the Encourage Coaching Conversation. This approach focuses on the other half of Dr. Kerr's formula: A coachee's *motivation* to take on a challenge and perform to his or her potential. Of course, the terms *motivate* and *encourage* are not synonymous. According to dictionary.com, to motivate someone is to "provide someone with a motive for doing something," whereas to encourage someone is to "give support, confidence, or hope to someone." Let's unpack each of these terms to discover how best to apply them.

Motivation

The whole question of what truly motivates people, at work and in other contexts, has been widely studied for many decades. Most readers are probably familiar with Abraham Maslow and his "Hierarchy of Needs" theory.[47] Maslow argued that we are motivated to meet basic needs such as survival and safety before higher level needs, ultimately including "self-actualization" or the full realization of one's talents and potential, become salient.

While Maslow's theory applies across virtually all contexts, a contemporary of his, the psychologist Frederick Herzberg, studied the question of what motivates people specifically at work.[48] His research resulted in his widely taught Hygiene-Motivator, or Two-factor, theory of job satisfaction. In a nutshell, Herzberg found two sets of variables that are related to what motivates us at work.

One set of variables, which Herzberg referred to as the "Hygiene" factor, consists of *tangible* aspects of one's work experience, such as company policies, work conditions, salary, status, and security.

---
[47] Maslow, "A Theory of Human Motivation."
[48] Herzberg, *The Motivation to Work.*

If anything related to these variables is considered fundamentally inadequate — employees are not making enough money to make ends meet, for instance – they will be dissatisfied. Once these needs are met to at least an adequate level, however, providing even more in these areas will not truly motivate employees.

The other set of variables, which Herzberg referred to as the "Motivator" factor, consists of more *intangible* aspects of one's work experience, such as achievement, recognition, the work itself, responsibility, advancement, and growth. Based on Herzberg's research, these are the things that truly motivate people at work.

Much more recently, thought leader Daniel Pink has arrived at a few conclusions that are consistent with and build upon what earlier researchers such as Maslow and Herzberg argued.[49] Pink's point of view is that money, which is perhaps the best example of a "Hygiene" variable in Herzberg's theory, is indeed a motivator at work, but that the best strategy when it comes to pay is to "get compensation right – and then get it out of sight."[50] In other words, if someone's pay is "broken," it should be fixed. But once it's at least fair and reasonable, there are other variables that truly motivate people.

Pink then argues that three key factors — autonomy, mastery, and purpose – are the things that truly motivate people at work. And while these are not exactly the same as Maslow's notion of "self-actualization" or Herzberg's "Motivator" factor, one thing all these "true motivators" have in common is that they are intangible.

Let us put it this way. If you are employed, right now you may be able to open your wallet and see and touch the paper currency and health

---

[49] Pink, *Drive*.
[50] Ibid., 170.

insurance card that are in there – both thanks to your job (unless, of course, you live in a country with universal health care). What you can't see or touch, however, are things like the freedom you have to do your job, your belief in your company's larger purpose, and your sense that you are growing and realizing your full potential.

The bottom line is that tangible variables like pay are important, but only to a certain extent. Once people *feel* like their more basic needs are being met to at least a sufficient degree in tangible ways, their deeper needs must be met in more intangible ways. And that's where *encouragement* enters the picture.

Encouragement

Alongside autonomy, purpose, and self-actualization, encouragement – especially from one's manager or coach – is a critical intangible motivator. In fact, the importance of encouragement seems to be getting more and more attention these days, for at least a couple of reasons.

First, research in the area of Positive Psychology helps build the case for the importance of encouragement in the workplace. Among the literature in this area from luminaries such as Martin Seligman[51] and Tal Ben-Shahar,[52] is a good article from Emma Seppala and Kim Cameron that discusses the application of Positive Psychology principles in the work environment.[53]

According to research both conducted and cited by Seppala and Cameron, there is a strong relationship between how *positive* employees believe their work culture is and how *productive* they are. And key qualities of a positive work culture include things like caring

---
[51] Seligman, "PERMA and the Building Blocks of Well-Being."
[52] Ben-Shahar, and Angus, *The Joy of Leadership*.
[53] Seppala and Cameron. "Proof That Positive Work Cultures."

for others, providing support, avoiding blame, forgiving mistakes, inspiring people, emphasizing the meaningfulness of work, and expressing gratitude to others. These are, of course, all things that a coach can do, and we believe they nicely capture the essence of the Encourage Coaching Conversation.

Another recent idea that supports the importance of encouragement in the workplace is the concept of Strengths-Based Development. A good example of research in this area can be found in Gallup's "State of the American Manager" report from 2017. One of the key findings from the very large study cited in this report is that there is a strong, positive correlation between the extent to which employees think their managers focus on their strengths (or positive characteristics) and their level of engagement. This dovetails with the finding – now well established in the management literature – that there is a strong relationship between employee engagement and performance, at both the individual and organizational levels.

In short, while encouragement from managers is not the only thing that motivates employees, it is certainly one key driver of outcomes like engagement and, ultimately, productivity and performance. And managers who see their job as being a good coach, who focus on encouragement as one key form of coaching, and who are effective in this area, are likely to have employees who are motivated and, thus, higher performing than their less motivated counterparts. This, then, begs the question: What does encouragement look and sound like?

What the Encourage Conversation Involves

As we delve further into the question of what an Encourage Coaching Conversation involves, we need to make one important prefatory note. As we explained in detail in Chapter 5, "The Coaching

Context," we believe that there are two aspects of the Coaching Context that relate to the motivation of the coachee – namely, confidence and commitment.

While both of these variables are fundamental to a coachee performing to his or her potential, the way to *encourage* somebody will vary significantly depending on whether a coach is trying to increase the individual's confidence, commitment, or both. Indeed, throughout the remainder of this chapter, it will likely be quite apparent whether a given approach to encouragement will be focused more on building confidence or on building commitment.

Seeking First to Understand

One of the thought leaders in this area whom we particularly admire is Dr. Rob Fazio, Managing Partner at OnPoint Advising. Dr. Fazio coined the term "Motivational Currency" to get at the idea that each of us is motivated by different things, and the effective leader or coach will be skilled at assessing what an individual's true motivators are and then adapting his or her approach to motivating someone accordingly.[54] Moreover, Fazio has identified four basic motivators:

- **PERFORMANCE,** meaning that one thrives on taking on challenges and exceeding expectations
- **PEOPLE**, which refers to a focus on how others are impacted by a given decision or action
- **POWER,** which puts a premium on being influential with others
- **PURPOSE,** which involves a longing for meaning in one's work and a desire to contribute to something bigger than just making a profit

---

[54] Fazio, *Simple Is the New Smart.*

All people are motivated by all these things, of course – but to varying degrees. And because people are wonderfully diverse, a good coach will begin any attempt to encourage someone by reflecting on and perhaps even exploring the question: What is this person truly motivated by?

A wise saying that gets at this important prerequisite to effectively encouraging others was provided decades ago by Stephen Covey in his classic book *The Seven Habits of Highly Effective People.* Covey argued that highly effective people "seek first to understand, then to be understood." We think this is an excellent guideline in general, and we believe – and our research supports – that it's particularly important when you are having an Encourage conversation.

In fact, when we asked Best Coach Garry Ridge what he thinks the key is to effectively encouraging somebody, he paused, pointed to a whiteboard behind him in his office, and drew our attention to one of the two phrases he had written there: "Ask, don't tell." (He gave credit for this aphorism to Frances Hesselbein, former CEO of the Girl Scouts of the USA and a prolific author in the field of leadership.)

When we asked if he could say a bit more about this advice, he said, "We're very bad listeners, and that's something we need to be better at, and people are *encouraged* when people listen to them." He then told us about a conversation he had had with Hesselbein, during which she shared the nugget to "Think first and speak last."

He went on to claim that most people tend to do the opposite of these things: They tell, rather than ask; and they speak first and think last. Our experience is generally consistent with Garry's. When you are seeking to encourage someone, however, it is better to think first and speak last for maximum positive impact.

A good example comes from Best Coach and former San Francisco Giants Manager Bruce Bochy. During our interview about effective coaching practices, he said, "If you're going to solve a problem or motivate someone, you need to figure out what the issue is." He then recounted a situation in which a player was "playing a bit nervous" and just wasn't himself. Bruce brought him into his office and said, "I don't know what's going on, and I can't help if I don't know what's up." The player opened up, and it turned out something outside the game was affecting his confidence and thus his performance on the baseball field. Once Bruce knew what the issue was, he got the player some help, and his performance improved.

This example may seem like a case where the best course of action was obvious, but we don't think so. In fact, we can think of several courses of action that a less effective coach might have taken. The coach could have put the player on the field and hoped he worked it out. The coach could have benched the player. The coach could have told the player exactly what he should do in order to turn things around.

But Bruce is not a future Hall of Fame major league baseball manager for nothing. He resisted the temptation to take the easier or more obvious path; instead, he engaged with the player in order to find out what the real issue was. Then, and only then, could Bruce and the San Francisco Giants organization take the right steps to address the true source behind the waning performance. This is not what all coaches do, but it is what *great* coaches do.

Expressing Appreciation

Another form of encouragement is to simply affirm that others are doing well and to express that you appreciate their efforts and/or contributions. This, in turn, boosts their confidence and thus helps them perform to their potential.

A story to illustrate this comes from one of our coauthors, who has played drums since he was eight years old and currently is one of the drummers at a large, contemporary church in the San Diego area. And one of the things that makes this church "contemporary" is its music. Most if not all of the musicians in the worship band play or have played in rock bands, some at a pretty high level.

As of the writing of this story, our coauthor-drummer had played three church services over the course of the weekend, and for two of the three services, a guest guitarist had sat in – a member of the worship band from one of the most well-known churches in the world when it comes to contemporary church music.

Now, while our coauthor has played drums for a long time and can probably be considered at least decent (at a minimum, he certainly has put Malcolm Gladwell's 10,000 hours in on a drum kit), after listening to the guest guitarist during warm-ups, it was clear that the guest performer was an especially strong player; much more so, frankly, than our coauthor.

And, as with any type of context, collaborating with somebody who is at a higher level than yourself can have both a motivating effect (a desire to "rise to the occasion"), as well as potentially an anxiety-producing effect (a tendency to question whether you are really up to the task). Our coauthor was feeling both of these things.

It so happened that the guitarist was positioned on the stage right in front of our coauthor, and a little off to the side. And during the first of four songs in the early Sunday service, our coauthor did a "fill" (a drum roll in the middle of the song) that was somewhat difficult to execute well, and the guest guitarist turned around, smiled, and nodded at our coauthor.

Even though our coauthor has been playing drums for decades and had played countless services at this very church over the last ten years or so, there was something about that simple smile and nod of encouragement from a particularly credible source that had a notable effect on our coauthor's drumming for the remainder of that service, as well as the following one that morning.

One way of describing that effect is that it "unleashed" something in the drummer – the drummer's full potential. You see, as with many skills, it's hard to play drums – or any instrument – to your full potential if you are playing while feeling nervous, tense, or apprehensive. And we believe the relationship between confidence (or, put differently, lack of apprehension) and performance exists whether it's a musician playing drums, a baseball player at the plate, or an executive on a stage speaking to a large group of employees.

Put simply, to perform to one's potential in any area, it's important to not only have the skill, but also the motivation and confidence, to perform well. And sometimes, a simple gesture of affirmation – even a brief, non-verbal gesture such as a nod and a smile from a fellow musician – can boost a coachee's confidence significantly and help unleash his or her full potential.

To further illustrate the importance of expressing appreciation as a form of the Encourage Coaching Conversation, we turn once again to Best Coach, Dr. Mark Brouker. Mark explained to us that a security force is assigned to every military hospital. At one point, when he was the commanding officer at Bremerton Naval Hospital in

Washington, active-duty members who had been providing security for VIPs in Afghanistan (including General Stanley McChrystal, the retired US Army four-star general best known for his command of Joint Special Operations Command in the mid-2000s) returned from that exciting deployment and had the new job of providing security at Bremerton.

Military hospitals need to conduct periodic security drills, and one was scheduled at Bremerton. The recently returned active-duty members had an idea for one that, according to Mark, would have been great for Kabul but was "way over the top" for a stateside hospital. The proposed drill even included a simulated terrorist running around the hospital complex with security team members chasing him with M16 rifles. Mark realized that he "needed to let them know that it was overkill, *but without discouraging them.*"

That last phrase is key. A less emotionally intelligent leader-coach might just say, "We are not going to use this approach; it's way too complex and involved for what we need here." But Mark is both very technically competent and very emotionally intelligent, and he immediately realized the importance of offering an encouraging word to these highly trained and well-intentioned professionals.

He reflected on where the "over the top" idea was coming from and realized that, given the impressive and laudable service of these active-duty members, there was certainly something quite praiseworthy in what they had come up with. Therefore, as Mark recounted the story to us, "I told them how impressive their proposed drill was – *because it was!*"

Mark carefully chose his words to express his sincere appreciation for their effort. Then, and only then, did he move on to trying to help them understand that the context at the Bremerton Naval Hospital was different from what they were accustomed to in Afghanistan. And throughout this interaction, the driving idea in the front of his mind was, "I just didn't want to *discourage* them."

Explaining the Why

The notion of "starting with why" was popularized by Simon Sinek,[55] whose essential point is that people don't buy a product or service, or buy into an idea or cause, because of *what* it does or *how* it works. Rather, we buy into something because of its underlying cause or premise or rationale – because we *identify* with it, we feel *inspired* by it. In other words, because of the *why*.

We believe this idea very much applies in the coaching context. Indeed, Best Coach Dr. Dilcie Perez told us that when she is coaching somebody at the outset of some new project or initiative, she always starts with the why. Why would she do that? She explains that, "With some people, you can give them the *why* and they know where to go from there." And, she added, she has had moments when, by focusing on the vision and the why behind the vision, she has been excited by what people come back with . . . *especially* if she didn't tell them exactly what to do or how to do it.

Sometimes, starting with why as a form of encouragement is prospective, **as in,** "Here's why we are going to be doing this." At other times, it's retrospective, as in, "Here's why we have made the decision we have made." But in either case, helping people understand the *why* behind a course of action or decision can keep them feeling encouraged.

---

[55] Sinek, *Start with Why*.

To go back to Mark's example at Bremerton, beyond expressing appreciation for all the work the team responsible for coming up with the security drill had done, he said, "It was also important to help them understand the why behind the decision to use a less elaborate drill." Indeed, Mark noted that explaining the rationale for a decision is "under the umbrella of respect." In other words, if you help people understand *why* you are making decisions in an honest and transparent way, they will get it. In this example, Mark took the time to walk through the rationale for going in a different direction with an important decision, and this was another way of keeping the team members encouraged.

Instilling Confidence

Another form of encouragement that coachees may benefit from, and that may result in accelerated professional development and increased levels of performance, is simply an expression of confidence. And, over the course of our decades of collective experience as leadership development consultants, we have found that there is virtually no context in which a sincere expression of confidence in a team member is considered meaningless.

To illustrate, for several years, one of us served arguably the world's preeminent management consulting firm – a firm packed with Harvard and Stanford MBAs everywhere you look. In other words, it's the best of the best – at least when it comes to academic credentials, career opportunities, and the like.

And yet, for all the intelligence and accomplishment to be found within this company's walls, a telling term that is widely used by these professionals to describe themselves and one another is "insecure overachiever."

In other words, we might assume that because someone has an Ivy League education, or a very senior job, or a hefty salary, he or she must be exceedingly self-confident. And, to be sure, this is sometimes the case. For example, we once worked for a client where, when a division president was asked by a more junior person in a group setting what he was working on to improve as a leader, the president replied, "Well, you shouldn't mess too much with the Mona Lisa." No lack of self-confidence there!

It's our opinion, however, that the vast majority of professionals need or at least would benefit from some occasional reassurance that they are good and that they know what they are doing. Best Coach Darryl Albertson, who was CHRO at a company specializing in transportation and defense systems at the time when the following story took place, offered us a great example.

One of Darryl's direct reports – we'll call her Selena – had been a ballerina "in a previous life." Perhaps in part due to that background, she was a perfectionist and extremely hard on herself. At some point virtually every day she felt that she had failed or hadn't accomplished what she had hoped to. Darryl tried to help Selena see that her self-perceptions didn't match the perceptions of her coworkers, all of whom thought she was great. He consistently shed light on her accomplishments and reinforced that, when she did her best, it was almost always good enough.

Consistent with the idea that coaching often happens over a long period of time, Darryl said he coached Selena on her confidence issue for roughly a year, and over time she became happier in her role and less critical of herself. He believes his coaching also helped her with prioritization, work-life balance, and other related outcomes –

all as a result of effectively using an Encourage coaching approach consistently and over time.

An additional example comes from Best Coach Michelle DiTondo, who told us about a director-level person who reported to her when we interviewed her. This person was a good thinker and presenter, but she got nervous when presenting to senior leaders because of a risk she perceived regarding how such leaders might see her. The approach that Michelle used was to affirm that the director knew her material well, that opportunities to present to senior leaders were good for her, and that she (Michelle as the coach) was confident that her director-level coachee would do well. These sorts of words of encouragement can do wonders for a coachee who is feeling hesitant in a given context.

Celebrating Successes

Based on our research, one of the most important coaching behaviors is: *"Celebrates current successes with those responsible."* In other words, great coaches know which players on a team are most responsible for team accomplishments, and they do a good job of celebrating those successes with the team members who were involved. And if a team's success really is the product of the efforts of an entire team, which is often the case, the coach celebrates with the whole team.

Our experience working with one highly effective coach in particular illustrates the importance of this coaching behavior. This senior leader oversees a high-performing team of close to fifty people within a firm in the financial services sector. As part of a leadership coaching and team development engagement with us, he got feedback that he could perhaps do more to celebrate team successes.

This need was vividly demonstrated during a town hall meeting with the entire team, during which the leader went through his team's excellent performance from the previous year. There was a moment of silence, and then he said, "Well, I think that deserves a bit of a golf clap"– at which point he began clapping softly, with his dozens of subordinates following suit. The "celebration" lasted just a few seconds, and then they moved on to the next thing.

After getting a bit more feedback about how he could and perhaps should stretch a little farther in the direction of celebrating accomplishments, the leader went out of his way at a similar event a year later to publicly praise a few team members for specific, significant contributions. This sort of thing increases the level of confidence and commitment among team members, and we think adding this dimension to his coaching approach has made him an even more effective leader. He still occasionally recognizes great team success with a polite golf clap – but we will keep working with him on that.

Clarifying Incentives and Consequences

Sometimes, the main thing a leader needs to do to encourage team members to take their performance to the next level is to clarify exactly what the incentives are for taking a certain course of action, and/or what the consequences are of not doing so. One of our Best Coaches, Mike Twyman, shared this: "I always tell my direct reports, 'You can't get promoted unless you have a successor.'" He also noted that, "Sometimes I'm very directive in saying, 'Look, you should take this job.'"

He went on to provide a great firsthand example. He once supervised a high-potential person who was an excellent business developer but wanted to be a manager. His organization had a need overseas, and Mike was very direct in telling his employee, "If you take this job, you'll get experience managing a P&L, and when you come back to the states, you will be at the director level." The direct report did what Mike was telling him he should do, and it all worked out as Mike indicated it would.

Creating a Safety Net

Much as an acrobat with an actual safety net is willing to try more challenging stunts, a coachee with a metaphorical safety net may be willing to take on more challenging tasks. When it comes to coaching, this metaphorical safety net may take at least two different forms.

Sometimes, a coach can reassure a coachee that the coach will be right in the middle of a situation in order to help support the coachee in real-time in case something starts to go wrong. In the case of Luke's participation in the public earnings call cited in Chapter 7, the coach (in this case, the company's CEO) was in the room from which the leaders were participating in the call, and when things started to go awry, the coach was right there to nonverbally communicate to the coachee that he needed to course correct. As mentioned when this example was introduced, while some Explain coaching would have been helpful, the fact that the CEO was there to support his direct report when there was a problem kept things from being as bad as they could have been.

The second form of metaphorical safety net is more psychological. In this case, if a coach is able to reassure a coachee that it's OK in a given situation to struggle, or even fail, as long as the coachee learns from the experience, that can create the sense of essentially having a safety net below.

One way of understanding how this works is by turning to Stanford psychologist Carol Dweck, who distinguishes between having a "fixed mindset" versus a "growth mindset."[56] Among other things, someone with a relatively fixed mindset tends to shy away from more challenging assignments for fear of failing, whereas someone with more of a growth mindset tends to embrace more challenging assignments and sees failure as a part of the learning process.

Best Coach Dilcie Perez put it this way: "When you normalize challenges and mistakes and help people realize all of that is just part of the process, it frees them up." She further explained, "I don't like the term 'failure.'" Instead, she chooses to laugh at herself and at challenging situations – all of which helps others feel more comfortable with taking on tough assignments.

To further illustrate, the father of one of our coauthors worked in home construction when our coauthor was growing up. On occasion, his father would take him to a job site and allow him to help with plastering walls. To reassure his son that he didn't need to do it perfectly, the father used to say, "There's nothing you can screw up that I can't fix." This, we believe, is a great example of a coach providing a psychological safety net for his coachee.

Lighting a Fire

One thing we have tried to emphasize throughout this book is the idea that effective coaching is sometimes warm and fuzzy, and sometimes it's not. Sometimes it's G-rated, and sometimes it's PG-13 or even R-rated. In other words, there are "textbook" notions of coaching such as "What are your goals? How might you get there?" and then there are the ways in which highly effective coaches actually

---

[56] Dweck, *Mindset*.

coach in real life. We are not saying that there's no overlap between the two; we're just saying that to frame coaching as a type of behavior that's always calm and measured is to ignore the reality that at times, successful coaches use approaches that are anything but placid.

Of course, this reality is probably more pronounced in some contexts than in others, and the sports context probably comes most readily to mind when we think of environments in which highly effective coaches get, shall we say, a bit animated.

Best Coach Bruce Bochy gave us a great example of this. Early in his tenure as manager of the San Francisco Giants, he saw some behaviors among the team he had inherited that he found unacceptable. As he described it, some players were being petty; they weren't "doing things right" by Major League Baseball standards; there were factions in the clubhouse; and so on. So, after one particularly uninspired performance on the baseball field, Bruce went into the clubhouse, grabbed a bat, and proceeded to destroy a flat screen TV.

That got the players' attention! And within a few years, the Giants, with Bruce at the helm, had won a World Series. Followed by another one two years later. And then a third two years after that.

Now, the transformation from a struggling ball club with some dysfunction in the clubhouse to a three-time world-champion organization in a hyper-competitive environment took years and involved a wide range of actions, not only on Bruce's part but also on the part of the rest of the Giants' leadership. But we would venture to say that Bruce's expressing, in no uncertain terms, that certain types of behavior were unacceptable was probably a big part of the turnaround of this team and its eventual rise to the pinnacle of success in its field.

When to Have the Encourage Conversation

You should initiate an Encourage Coaching Conversation when the Coaching Cue of "hesitant" appears and the coachee's Central Issue is lack of or need for confidence and/or commitment. If either of these cues are present, there are a few approaches you can take to aid the coachee in gaining or regaining the motivation to face the task or challenge.

Best Coach Kevin Freiberg explains it well: "When someone is quite competent but is insecure, you should encourage that person to trust his or her ability – to give oneself permission to not be doubtful, and to give something his or her best try." Kevin's emphasis on the importance of "small wins" applies here, so that the coachee's confidence gets built and he or she gains more and more of what we might call "mojo."

Sometimes, this type of conversations involves encouraging coachees to revisit a time in the past when they were faced with a task, challenge, or obstacle similar to what is currently causing them to feel nervous. Is there an instance when they did it and did it well? If so, what strengths did they use to get it done? If, on the other hand, they don't have a successful example to revisit, then what did they learn when they didn't do it well? In either case, what can the coachee leverage from these past examples to help in the current situation?

Another way to create thoughtful dialogue as a part of an Encourage Coaching Conversation is to ask the coachee to think about someone who has successfully completed the task, or who successfully overcame the challenge or obstacle in question. What traits, behaviors, or skills did the coachee observe in this individual that led to success? How might the coachee utilize a similar approach?

In yet other coaching contexts, we believe the coachee's Central Issue is that he or she needs some form of *assurance.* Sometimes, this assurance is intended to address the coachee's relative lack of confidence. A highly credible manager, for example, may be very well-positioned to offer some assurance to a direct report that he or she really does "have what it takes" to excel in a given situation.

At times, this can work for external coaches, as well. One of us once coached a relatively senior leader who was working on his executive presence. The leader was extremely well-educated, intelligent, knowledgeable, and accomplished; however, he was also extremely introverted (or "painfully shy," as his manager put it). This resulted in him staying relatively quiet in large meetings, for instance, instead of confidently stating his point of view.

Since our coauthor had worked extensively in the coachee's firm and had a pretty good sense of how strong other firm leaders were relative to the leader he was coaching, he attempted to offer some assurance. "Look," he said at one point, "you are Harvard-educated, rocket scientist smart, and respected by virtually everyone in this firm who knows you." When we think of the word "encourage," we often think of compliments and soft support, but sometimes it needs to be more of a challenge and "kick in the pants." In such a situation, essentially challenging the person, relative to his or her skills and abilities, may get the person to step up to a challenge that he or she otherwise might be feeling reluctant about.

In other coaching contexts, the purpose of any assurance that you as the coach can offer is to address any potential lack of commitment on the part of the coachee. Again, this type of assurance can be offered both by internal coaches, such as someone's manager, and by external coaches.

To illustrate this idea, we'd like to refer to one of the best-known business leaders in history – the late Steve Jobs, co-founder of Apple and the company's CEO during two different pivotal stretches in the company's history. When we work with groups of leaders, the "Steve Jobs question" sometimes comes up. This question is usually some variation of the following: "All this stuff you are saying sounds good, but what about Steve Jobs? He apparently was a jerk, and yet look how well his company has done."

We believe this is a fair question, and we also believe there are several good answers. For example, while it appears to be true, based on numerous biographical accounts, that Jobs' behavior toward his colleagues and employees was not always the model of respectful leadership, we must keep in mind that he was Apple's CEO, then he was fired from that position by Apple's Board of Directors – and then he *stepped back into* the CEO role at Apple years later. And, by most accounts, he learned some things during the interim (through his experience leading NeXT and Pixar). In short, Steve Jobs 1.0 at Apple was arguably quite different from Steve Jobs 2.0 at Apple.

However, there is something else about Jobs that we think is important to keep in mind – and this is something that relates directly to the idea of providing assurance to people. As Jon Katzenbach puts it in his article on Steve Jobs in Strategy + Business[57], Jobs "always challenged teams – from those involved in the early product efforts led by Apple cofounder Steve Wozniak onward – to reach beyond the possible." Katzenbach, like others who have studied Jobs, then

---

[57] Katzenbach, "The Steve Jobs Way."

notes that this approach worked much better for some Apple people than others (for example, the A-Players vs. the B- or C-Players).

Yet, Katzenbach's observation gets at the essence of something Jobs was exceptional at – creating a vision of an Apple that was changing the world, inspiring people to want to be a part of that and assuring people that they were capable of great things. So, while we acknowledge that Jobs, by all accounts, had some less-than-ideal qualities as a leader, one thing he apparently excelled at was a certain form of motivation that helped him lead one of the great companies in history.

To bring it back to our concept of the Central Issue, sometimes what the coachee needs is assurance. And sometimes, the assurance needed is that the coachee can do what is expected, and at other times the assurance needed is a sense that, by giving something his or her best effort, the coachee has a chance to be a part of something great.

The Trust Connection

We would like to make two final points about the Encourage Coaching Conversation. The first is that this type of conversation may be especially critical as part of a leader's coaching toolkit as the leader moves into more senior roles. The logic here is that as a leader moves up through the ranks, it is likely that he or she will increasingly be overseeing areas within the organization where people lower-down in the hierarchy have more technical expertise than the leader.

The Encourage Coaching Conversation, perhaps more than any other, has as a prerequisite, a trusting relationship between coach and coachee.

As Best Coach Matt Cole puts it, "I'm not an engineer, and in fact, I'm actually not that technically competent. So, when I'm talking with my engineering department, I may turn to a more motivational approach to coaching by asking how I can help, encouraging people who are making progress, thanking people for their efforts, and things like that." In other words, a leader may not always have the technical competence to be credible as an "advice-giver," but a good coach can always develop the interpersonal competence to be credible as an "encourager of people."

Our second point as part of the wrap-up to this chapter is that the Encourage coaching conversation, perhaps more than any other, requires substantial trust between the coach and coachee. After all, this is the type of conversation that may get into a coachee's fears, anxieties, and self-doubt. So, we agree with Best Coach Kevin Freiberg's advice when he says an important aspect of this type of coaching conversation is "letting the coachee know you are there for him or her." After all, as Kevin explains, "It's hard for people to be vulnerable if they don't know you are really there for them."

In practice, this may take several forms: Literally being available to talk when a coachee needs you; really hearing the coachee's concerns and expressing empathy; authentically expressing your confidence in the coachee; and periodically telling the coachee some version of "I'm here for you." But regardless of how you translate this important principle into behavior, the larger point is this: The Encourage Coaching Conversation, perhaps more than any other, has as a prerequisite a trusting relationship between coach and coachee.

Trust is established over time and through many small gestures and interactions. As such, the level of trust will vary between any two people, and it may also vary over time. As discussed earlier, we like to equate this to the metaphor of having a "trust bank account" with each person with whom you interact: Credits to this bank account will increase the level of trust, while debits will decrease or erode the level of trust. So, we leave you with two questions as we conclude this chapter: How would you assess the level of trust you have with those you lead and coach? And what could you do to increase the level of trust so that your encouragement is well-received?

The EMPOWER Coaching Conversation

chapter **10**

---

*"Control leads to compliance.
Autonomy leads to engagement."*

~ DANIEL PINK – Author and speaker

THERE COMES A TIME (AT LEAST IF THINGS GO WELL) when a coachee has become proficient and successful enough to warrant a certain level of latitude or autonomy to approach a responsibility in the way that he or she thinks is best. Best Coach Elisabet Hearn calls this approach "taking off the training wheels." And, while we grant that this analogy is a bit paternalistic, it vividly illustrates what it looks like for a coach to give a coachee significant freedom and responsibility on the task at hand.

Recall from the Encourage chapter that Daniel Pink proposes that one of the three key factors that truly motivate people is *autonomy*, meaning the latitude to be relatively self-directed at work. We agree, but only when an employee has sufficient competence and commitment to be able to excel when given significant latitude. To give lots of autonomy to somebody who lacks both skill and confidence would be, in our opinion, grossly irresponsible on the part of the coach, and it would likely lead to a poor outcome.

However, when a coachee has sufficient ability and motivation to be able to handle lots of autonomy in a given context, we think the Empower Coaching Conversation is the appropriate approach. So, for the remainder of this chapter, we will wrestle with the question: What does an effective Empower Coaching Conversation involve? And, more specifically, how can you provide sufficient structure to give a coachee an excellent chance at success, without the coaching straying into micromanagement (essentially using an Explain or Explore approach with someone who is high in terms of Confidence, Competence, and Commitment)?

Empowerment Gone Awry

Let us begin our discussion of effective empowerment by offering an anecdote to illustrate what this approach looks like when it is *not* used in the right type of context. This example comes from Gloria (not her real name), a mentee and past colleague of one of our coauthors who had just started her doctoral program and was offered a paid research assistantship with two professors she had been looking forward to working with.

Unfortunately, Gloria's onboarding process provided little clarity regarding the work she was expected to do, and then she found herself put in charge of an ongoing research project that involved collecting data across California. While an extremely competent and confident person in general, she quickly became discouraged with the work and frustrated by the lack of guidance. Meetings with her research leads were frequently changed at the last minute or canceled altogether, and the leads were distracted with other obligations and often didn't know the basic procedures themselves.

Gloria began to doubt herself and question both her own initiative and her ability. Meanwhile, more assignments and responsibilities piled up. At one point she wondered if the professors were testing her to see if she was up to the job. Without the basic foundation that an Explain approach would have provided, she was unable to move effectively into a position of empowerment. She went from being enthusiastic about the actual work being done to a place where she was fearful, anxious, and constantly questioning herself.

This is an example of where coaching really fell short. After months of not having proper guidance, Gloria took the initiative to schedule a meeting with the professors overseeing her work to decide if she was going to continue the assignment. They listened and were receptive to her concerns, and they were able to put together a plan to become more involved in training her, and to set her up with the tools she would need to own the project for herself.

In Gloria's case, at the outset the lead professors knew she was motivated, and they knew she did excellent work. As a result, they used a variation of the Empower approach that is, unfortunately, all too common in situations like this, and which we *don't* recommend. We call it the "dump and run" approach, and as Gloria's story illustrates, it can actually cause an extremely capable and motivated coachee to lose confidence and commitment. Bottom line: Recall Dr. Steve Kerr's formula (which we introduced in Chapter 5) that Ability x Motivation = Performance. Good coaching should result in higher levels of each of these two factors related to performance.

But, consistent with the Hippocratic Oath – "First, do no harm" – we *never* want a coachee to *lose* any amount of motivation (and possibly even ability) as a result of poor coaching. And that's exactly what happened in Gloria's case.

As Best Coach Kevin Freiberg explains it: "Empowering someone when he or she isn't ready for it is a crime; it's unfair to the person who is looking to you for coaching." We agree. It wasn't so much a case of Gloria "not being ready" to be empowered as "not being properly informed" by the professors supervising her about the assignment and expectations.

At the same time, however, we also agree with Kevin's point that "Turning someone loose is a great way to help that person continue to grow, even more than when you continue to be hands-on." So, let's address the question of what appropriately "turning someone loose" really looks like.

What the Empower Conversation Involves

The Empower coaching approach begins with a coach delegating some sort of responsibility to a coachee. According to our research for this book, one of the top predictors of overall coaching effectiveness is: *"Delegates responsibilities to those who are competent to handle them."* Of course, the coach must exercise excellent judgment, both in terms of whom to delegate to, and also with regard to the approach to use in truly empowering someone.

The point about an effective Empower conversation that Gloria's story clearly (though unfortunately) illustrates is this: Effective empowerment is an *active* process, not a passive one. In other words, "Empower" is not synonymous with "abdicate." Rather, it is a mindful, deliberate approach intended to set up a coachee for success by providing the right type and amount of structure. And we think this approach involves five key questions: Why, What, Who, How, and When? We will address each in turn.

Why?

The first question to ask before delegating something and essentially empowering the coachee to proceed as he or she sees fit is: *Why* are you delegating and empowering? In our view, there are two basic reasons for a coach to empower someone else to do something.

First, it may be good for a coach to delegate something to a coachee so that the coach can focus on other, higher-level duties. Indeed, research in the field of leadership[58] consistently indicates that one of the top derailers of otherwise promising leaders is an *inability to let go.*

This is understandable, since many coaches were once players, either literally or figuratively, in the area in which they are now coaching people. And, there's a good chance somebody has been tapped to coach others because he or she is seen as having been at least reasonably competent in that area. As a result, a coach likely has a preferred way of doing things and may be reluctant to hand off certain duties and/or to give people latitude to handle such duties as they see fit. And oftentimes, that's for good reason. But sometimes, in our experience, it's because the coach is what we call the "perfectionist control freak."

There are, of course, many problems with a coach being seen as a perfectionist control freak: Coachees find it very disengaging; it can stifle creativity and perhaps even thwart improved approaches to doing things; it can cause coach burnout; and many others. But a key problem with failing to effectively delegate and empower others is that if you are too far into the weeds, so to speak, it limits your capacity to focus on higher-level responsibilities that may be critical at your level.

Best Coach Garry Ridge spends an unusual amount of time focused on the WD-40 culture. He writes extensively about it, he frequently

---

[58] de Vries and Engellau, *Handbook of Leadership Theory and Practice.*

speaks about it, and he delights in taking visitors on tours of the company's headquarters, where interesting cultural artifacts are on display everywhere. If Garry were not exceptional at recognizing high levels of Confidence, Competence, and Commitment in his senior leaders and empowering them accordingly, there's no way he could devote himself as fully as he does to responsibilities he is uniquely positioned to fulfill, both based on his position and also based on his values and signature strengths as a leader.

A second good reason for a coach to empower others when possible and appropriate is that the coachee may grow and develop from taking on whatever the duty is. True, there are times when coaches simply need to get something off their plate in order to free up capacity to focus on other details that must be attended to at their level. However, if coachees feel that they are *only* being asked to take on mundane, lower-level, decidedly unglamorous tasks, they will likely experience disengagement, and the coach will almost certainly miss opportunities to create even higher levels of competence and confidence.

To return once again to Daniel Pink and one of the ideas from his excellent book *Drive*, two of the key factors that motivate people are *autonomy* and *mastery*. In other words, people like to be given at least a reasonable amount of freedom to perform duties in the way they think will work best, and they also like to feel that they are increasingly mastering the work they are responsible for. Strategic and effective empowerment can accomplish both of these purposes, depending on the remaining aspects of your approach to delegation and empowerment.

What?

The second question to ask before delegating something and essentially empowering the coachee to proceed as he or she sees fit is:

What are you empowering the coachee to do? In our view, there are two basic levels of empowerment: 1) empowering someone to take on and "run with" an *entire project or duty;* and 2) empowering someone to handle one or more *specific tasks* that fall within some broader project or duty. Let us provide a brief example of each, both from Best Coach Bruce Bochy.

In our interview, Bruce said, "I would let my bench coach manage a game in certain situations." If Bruce thought that was the best thing for the team in a given game, and/or the best thing for a given coach in light of Bruce's efforts to develop that individual, he handed over responsibility for an entire game.

However, empowering a coachee doesn't always involve completely delegating an entire duty; sometimes it just means that, in a given situation, the coach decides to hand off a specific task or defer to a coachee on a specific decision. To illustrate this, Bruce noted, "Sometimes, I would send my pitching coach to the mound to see if we should leave a pitcher in. Or, we would be considering which reliever to put in, and the pitching coach might ask, 'Who do you want?' and I would say, 'Who do *you* want?'" There are times when the position coach is in a better position to make that call than the manager. When that was the case, he would empower a member of his coaching staff to make a specific decision.

In short, part of the active aspect of coaching is to be mindful and deliberate about exactly what you are empowering a coachee to take on. By the end of an Empower Coaching Conversation, it should be clear to the coachee exactly what he or she is being asked to do, and what he or she will therefore be accountable for.

Who?

We noted in Chapter 5 that, according to Dr. Steve Kerr, a coach must consider and be able to positively influence two key factors in order to maximize the performance of the person he or she is coaching. Kerr referred to these two factors in his Performance formula as Ability and Motivation. Others refer to these factors as "skill" and "will."

We have broken motivation, or will, down into two different categories: confidence and commitment, both of which are detailed in Chapter 5 (The Coaching Context). These two factors, combined with the coachee's competence to deal with the responsibility at hand, comprise the coachee-specific factors you need to consider in deciding: 1) whether to delegate an assignment to someone, and 2) the extent to which you should empower the coachee.

From our perspective, the key is to ensure that the coachee has *sufficient* Confidence, Competence, and Commitment to more or less take ownership of the duty that he or she is being empowered to take on. This does not mean that the coachee would tackle the assignment exactly the way you would, although certain things do need to be handled in a specified way (for instance, issues related to compliance guidelines and the like). This also does not necessarily mean that the coachee would tackle the assignment as *effectively* as you would, though sometimes the coachee will actually do a *better* job than you!

Indeed, great coaches are highly attuned to and appreciative of the fact that they may well have direct reports who know more than they do about areas they are ultimately responsible for. As Best Coach Darryl Albertson put it, "As you move up in any organization you lead people who know more than you."

Darryl went on to cite a personal example, explaining that he had a benefits leader who knew more than he did on the subject. "I have had some exposure to benefits, but I'm not a benefits expert. However, I still had to play the leader role in order to give her organizational context and to provide resources."

Ultimately, according to Darryl, the benefits leader was essentially leading him, including suggesting steps he could take that would help the benefits function. Practically speaking, Darryl says, the way empowerment looked in this situation was fewer one-on-one meetings and more conversations that were less focused on addressing performance issues and more focused on information-sharing and long-term career development.

Once again, all of this requires that you be mindful about your approach to empowering someone. When it comes to the question of *whom* the coach empowers in a given area, Best Coach Hina Asad has some good advice: "I think about a situation where the person I'm working with has been successful in the past, and I help them tap into that as an example to empower them and boost their confidence." Empowerment is an *active process,* in part involving the deliberate determination of whether or not someone is a good fit for a given responsibility.

Another important factor, in addition to the coachee's Confidence, Competence, and Commitment, is his or her capacity to take on a given duty at a particular point in time. Quite simply, as part of an Empower Coaching Conversation, you should ask questions like, "What else do you have on your plate right now?" and "How much time do you have to take this assignment on, considering other priorities you have?"

If the coachee is fully able and willing to take something on, but is attempting to beg off by saying, "Just not right now!" the coach risks frustrating the employee by making the handoff anyway. It could create a work-life imbalance for a period of time, along with other less-than-optimal outcomes. In other circumstances, though, coachees just need to extend themselves beyond their comfort zone. All of these sorts of situations can be managed if you just ask a few thoughtful questions and respond accordingly.

How?

Now, to be sure, an Empower approach to coaching to some extent involves providing the coachee with a safe space to "dare to fail"– that is, to take a risk and, in some cases, to stumble and fall. As Best Coach Mary Watson puts it, "You have to allow room for failure, and you must be compassionate and understanding when someone you are coaching makes a mistake."

This does not mean you should provide the coachee with so little direction that he or she is basically set up to fail. As you read in the "Empowerment Gone Awry" story earlier in this chapter, that's exactly what the leaders in Gloria's case did, and if Gloria had not taken it upon herself to insist on additional structure, the program she's enrolled in might have lost an excellent student.

This "freedom to fail and learn" aspect of empowerment is an inoculation against people becoming disenfranchised or demotivated. As a coach, it is important for you to work toward a position of empowering people to have autonomy not only to *do* the work but also to figure out *how* to best do the work. Your coachees then get to own their work in a new way. Empowering people in their work does not mean leaving them on their own without a safety net. It does mean they are given the tools they need and some freedom to explore. Again, this is an active coaching technique and not a passive one.

In terms of creating a safe environment when empowering someone, our Best Coaches mentioned the need to know what might be intimidating for someone, such as constant doubt about their ability, not knowing whether they have the resources they will need, or not realizing they have will have "air cover" in case something goes wrong. Empowerment requires actual coaching conversations both before the empowerment occurs and while the empowerment is happening, so that coachees' confidence is built up to match their current and potential ability.

Once again, good counsel in this area comes from Best Coach Hina Asad, who said, "A leader needs to get rid of his or her fear around allowing someone to do a task on their own and also to provide a safety net." She says the approach she uses with her team is simply to say, "Before you call me, think it through!" The key here, according to Hina, is for the coach to assure coachees that you are there if they need help while you simultaneously seek to inspire and foster independence rather dependence in them.

Some additional wise counsel on how to actually empower someone effectively comes from another Best Coach, Elisabet Hearn, who suggests that "True empowerment should *enable* the other person to do what you are asking them to do, and this can be accomplished by asking questions like: Do you have the resources you need? Do you have the support you need? What else do you need? And what does success look like?" However, once a coachee has been as enabled as possible to succeed, Elisabet subscribes to the adage, "Try, learn, move on!"

When?

Once we had what we thought was a sound early version of our coaching model, but before the publication of this book, we started using our model in some of our client work – much of which involves helping leaders become more effective at coaching the people they lead. And, in an earlier version of this model, we included only Why, What, Who, and How in our description of the Empower Coaching Conversation.

Then, in one of our workshops, a leader asked, "Isn't it important to address the question of 'when,' as well?" After some discussion, we realized that she was right, and we added this question to our model. And, once again, this question gets at two different things. First, if you are handing off some sort of responsibility that has an actual deadline, it certainly makes sense to make that deadline clear. Second, it's often wise to think about milestones along the way rather than assuming that some deliverable which has been delegated to a coachee will be A+ work when presented on or shortly before the due date.

To illustrate, one of us was once in a role where he had responsibility for managing a layoff process that lasted the better part of a year. The goal he and his team had agreed on was that they wanted to make it the "best layoff possible," even though that may sound oxymoronic. One action toward that end was the team deciding to offer exceptional outplacement counseling to everyone who was being laid off.

Our coauthor gave this responsibility to a direct report, along with a deadline. But he failed to incorporate appropriate milestones into the project. As a result, when the deadline arrived and the direct report proposed an approach, including an outside outplacement resource, which unfortunately had significant flaws, there was relatively little time before implementation of the plan needed to begin. Our coauthor had to take the project back from the direct report and get to end-of-job on his own.

Our coauthor admits this was poor empowerment on his part for at least a couple of reasons. First, he didn't effectively confirm that the direct report had sufficient Confidence, Competence, and Commitment to complete the assignment. And second, failing to include appropriate milestones in the process kept him from having a way to monitor the direct report's progress. By the time it was clear that she was not going to be able to get the job done without some significant Explain and/or Explore coaching, it was too late, and our coauthor needed to pull the assignment back. Needless to say, this was not only less than ideal from an effectiveness point of view, but it was highly frustrating for the coachee as well – and understandably so!

In sum, an effective Empower Coaching Conversation involves addressing five basic questions for the coachee: Why, What, Who, How, and When. These are familiar, of course, because they are questions that journalists should ask themselves when investigating and writing a story. We think these questions can essentially serve as a checklist for any Empower conversation (see Figure 10.1). That is to say, if you put some thought into these questions before such a conversation and then make sure that answers to each of these questions are as clear as possible by the end of an Empower conversation, there's a pretty good chance you are setting the coachee up for success.

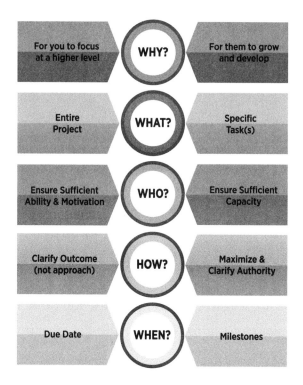

Figure 10.1 | *Empower Conversation Questions: A Checklist*

When to Have the Empower Conversation

You should initiate an Empower Coaching Conversation when the Coaching Cue of "success" is present and the coachee's Central Issue is lack of and/or need for autonomy. The key here is to ensure that the coachee feels *enabled and supported* to approach a situation in his or her own way.

Leveraging this approach to empower and enable subject matter experts will aid them with the direction, clarity, and information they need (when it is requested), in a supportive, autonomous way so they can continue moving forward and doing what they do best. Best Coach Ryan Fletcher explains: "For my employees with more experience than I have, I'm here to provide support, to help them if they have problems, and to give the approvals and direction to keep them going."

On the other hand, Best Coach Bruce Bochy provides a great reality check when it comes to empowering people. Bruce explained to us that while "It's such an important part of our game to delegate," he noted that, "There are times when I'm 100% sure of what I want to do, so I only delegate to them when I'm not." We think this is a great example of the difference between coaching in *theory* and coaching in *practice*.

In theory, as books like "You Already Know How to be Great"[59] suggest, people already have greatness within them, and the main thing a coach should be doing is finding ways to draw that greatness out. But in practice, there's a reason why Bruce Bochy is the Manager, and Garry Ridge is the CEO, and Mark Brouker is the Commanding Officer, and so on. And that reason is — *they know stuff their subordinates don't!*

We frankly love that Bruce acknowledged this reality in our conversation with him. He's a future Major League Baseball Hall of Fame Manager – and his Pitching Coach (as skilled and knowledgeable as he may be) – well, let's just say he probably isn't. So, if Bruce is certain that he knows what he wants to do in a given situation, it seems to us that it would be disingenuous and foolish (bordering on irresponsible) *not* to take responsibility for making the call. The same goes for you.

The Empowerment Challenge

One final point we would like to make about the Empower Coaching Conversation is that, in our experience, learning how to really

---

[59] Fine and Merrill, *You Already Know How to Be Great.*

empower others is one of the most significant challenges the leaders we work with face. Indeed, we have seen countless 360-degree feedback reports over the years in which the term "micromanager" appears – and it's generally not used as a term of endearment!

Best Coach Marshall Goldsmith refers to the practice of attempting to "add too much value" as a pitfall that many leaders fall into.[60] In fact, one of our firm's research questions in *How Leaders Improve* was: What were the most common "Central Issues" that our "most improved leaders" were working on? Some variation of "empowering others" was toward the top of the list.

We think this is related to the concept of credibility, which we discussed in Chapter 5. Often, an individual gets promoted from what one of our clients calls a "player" role into a "coach" (or "player-coach") role – largely because of technical competence and demonstrable character. Of course, the skills necessary to be a great *player* are not the same as the skills required to be a great *coach*. But since the individual's strengths and "value-add" over time have been more technical in nature, it's common for new coaches to continue to be too hands-on with regards to the technical aspects of what their team members do. The remedy for this pitfall? Empowering others to do their jobs versus doing it for them – provided, of course, the context is conducive to it.

---

[60] Goldsmith, and Reiter, *What Got You Here*.

The ELEVATE Coaching Conversation

chapter **11**

---

*"We cannot lower the mountain;
therefore, we must elevate ourselves."*

~ TODD SKINNER – Free climber

WHAT IMAGE DOES THE TERM "ELEVATE" CONJURE UP FOR YOU? Do you think of being at a high *elevation* up in the mountains? Do you think of being in an *elevator* riding to the top floor of a skyscraper? Do you think of being on a treadmill at a fitness center in order to *elevate* your heart rate? Something else?

When we came up with the name Elevate for our fifth type of coaching conversation, the image we had in mind was of a coach helping a coachee get to some new, higher level. Best Coach Kevin Freiberg expressed this idea very well when he said, "The end game for all coaching should be to *elevate* people, not just to get them to do their jobs sufficiently. If you don't want people to exceed their own sense of what they can do, then you should get out of coaching."

Kevin's comments get at a key distinction between the Elevate Coaching Conversation and the other four in our model – Explain, Explore, Encourage, and Empower. Those conversations deal with a coach's efforts to help a coachee perform to his or her potential *in a specific area.*

Indeed, if you look at the examples we cited throughout the last four chapters, you will notice that many if not most of them involve a coach focusing on a coachee's responsibility in a specific area. In one example, a business head used an Explain approach to help prepare a direct report to handle part of a town hall presentation. In another, a CEO used an Explore approach to help a direct report think through the best approach to improving performance measurements in the organization. In a third, a CHRO used an Encourage approach to help a direct report who had perfectionist tendencies understand that she was performing much better than she realized. And in yet another, a Major League Baseball manager described how he used Empower with his pitching coach to help him make a decision about which relief pitchers to use late in a game.

The Elevate Coaching Conversation is fundamentally different from those examples. The basic message being communicated from coach to coachee using this type of conversation is this: "You are demonstrating Confidence, Competence, and Commitment across the range of things you are responsible for, and you are performing extremely well; now, let's talk about how to get you to the next level."

Just what do we mean when we use the term "next level"? In some cases, this refers to an actual new role. Best Coach Debra Squyres, VP of Customer Success at Beamery, noted that when someone is performing well in his or her current role and has ambitions to move up, move laterally, or move into another area altogether (perhaps even with a different organization), her job as a coach is to ask questions. And the goal of each question is to get the coachee thinking about such matters as: What am I really interested in? What do I truly enjoy? What do I prefer to avoid? In the Elevate context, Squyres says she sees her role largely as "helping people uncover and then address their aspirations."

In other cases, "next level" may refer to something less tangible but nonetheless important, such as helping raise someone's profile within the organization. More tangible (and measurable) outcomes include improving skills or adding to one's set of skills. As Best Coach Kevin Freiberg explains it, "When done well, coaching is helping people go to places they may not have gotten to on their own."

As president of a division of a large defense contractor, Best Coach Mike Twyman says that in his environment it's common for really bright engineers to want to advance in their career. This gives him an opportunity to initiate what could best be described as an Elevate conversation.

In this type of conversation, he tends to ask lots of questions along the lines of: Where do you want to be? What are the logical paths to get you there? Do you want to stay on a more technical path? Do you want to run a business? And so on. As you'll recall, the Explore approach also involves asking lots of good questions. But the difference is that Explore questions generally have to do with how to address a particular issue or maximize one's performance in a given area, whereas Elevate questions are intended to get high-performing, high-potential employees thinking about where they want to go professionally, and how best to get there.

Our Best Coach Mike continued by saying that once he has a good sense of where the coachee wants to go, and he and the coachee have discussed options for getting there, the two of them will come up with a plan and agree on how they are going to follow through. Again, this sounds very much like an Explore conversation (and, in fact, the ISEE model we described in Chapter 8 might well be a helpful tool to use during this kind of Elevate conversation). The focus here, however, is on the coachee's potential *overall* and how to realize it, as opposed to his or her potential *in a given area* and how to maximize it.

In fact, we'd like to return to a point that we made in Chapter 4, which was that we readily acknowledge that our coaching model is similar in some ways to other existing models, especially the Situational Leadership model. As we explained, one of our goals is actually to extend on the Situational Leadership model in particular and, in so doing, to hopefully contribute to the literature in the field of leadership.

As we mentioned earlier, when we have used Situational Leadership in the past, one thing that often comes up is some variation of the question: "Hey, this model stresses that 'readiness' (a follower's 'skill' and 'will' or whatever terms are used in a given version of the model) is task-specific; what does the model say about somebody who is basically high in these dimensions *across the board?*"

Well, our Elevate coaching conversation is intended in part to address that very good question! Indeed, this is one of a number of things we have tried to do through our model to account for additional variables beyond what the Situational Leadership and other existing models address.

What the Elevate Conversation Involves

At its core, the Elevate coaching conversation has to do with talking with high-potential, high-performing people (commonly referred to as "hi-po" employees) about the ways in which they can get to a new level professionally. And this applies to all hi-po employees, whether they answer a phone, drive a forklift, or attend senior leader meetings in the boardroom. As Best Coach Darryl Albertson put it, "People at higher levels still want to grow and develop, get bigger titles, and make more of an impact." So, as this former executive-level leader explained, it's important for a coach in the organizational context to constantly be thinking about assignments that will help the high-performing person get to that next level.

And to be clear – Darryl was careful to clarify that the "next level" is not always a higher-level position on the organizational chart. It might just be a position or project that has more breadth to it or involves some other change that will help the hi-po employee further grow and develop. The key in these coaching discussions is that the coachee must trust that you really have his or her best interests in mind and that you are going to do what you say you are going to do. In other words, to use Darryl's language, it's important to have *credibility* – which, as discussed in Chapter 5, is an important part of the Coaching Context.

Knowing People's Goals and Aspirations

We often ask groups of leaders to think of the most effective leaders they have ever known, and to then reflect on the key things those leaders did that made them so effective. Almost invariably, people say that those leaders genuinely seemed to care about them – both professionally and personally.

Demonstrating care for others in a coaching situation involves having an interest in their personal lives and being flexible when they have legitimate non-work-related challenges they need to deal with. As President Theodore Roosevelt mused, "People don't care how much you know until they know how much you care!"

The section titled "Helping Someone Move Onward and Upward" later in this chapter provides some examples of how to care for coachees on a *personal* level. What we want to discuss at this point focuses on how a coach can care for people *professionally*, and this includes knowing what people's goals and aspirations are, and then helping them think through ways of accomplishing them. In fact, another key coaching behavior revealed through our research is: *"Demonstrates that he/she cares about the goals and aspirations of others."*

Although this seems like an obvious thing for coaches to demonstrate, we are frequently amazed by how little the leaders we work with actually know about the professional goals of the people they coach. In fact, the *lowest-rated* survey item in the biannual survey of managerial effectiveness conducted by one of our clients (a high-performing firm, by the way) had to do with leaders having coaching conversations with their employees to understand their broader career aspirations. So, a good starting place is simply to ask yourself: Do I actually know the professional goals and aspirations of the people I coach? If so, great! If not, ask them!

Matching Skills with Opportunities

Sometimes, the key to effective Elevate coaching is to make it a priority to really understand a given coachee's strengths and skills, and to be constantly thinking about opportunities that will allow them to sharpen those skills and apply them in a new way. For an example of this we return to our interview with Best Coach Darryl Albertson.

Darryl recounted the story of the time his company changed their Human Resources Information System to a sophisticated and widely used system called Workday. The complex implementation required that an in-house employee be assigned to manage the project and monitor the vendor relationship for a full year.

The person Darryl had in mind as the right candidate had the necessary technical expertise, yet when presented with the opportunity, the employee indicated it was not something he had thought of. So, Darryl met with him to discuss how the employee's skills would match up nicely with the project needs, and they also talked about the employee's career goals.

In that context, Darryl pointed out how implementing the system overall would give the employee experience across all aspects of HR and leverage his technical expertise. The individual ended up taking the assignment, and it was a great success. In fact, this company is now one of the most comprehensive users of Workday, and Darryl credits the coachee's great job with the implementation as the reason why.

To Darryl's assessment of the reasons for the project's success we would add that the positive outcome was also largely due to Darryl's skillful coaching, starting with matching the needs of the organization to the skills and aspirations of one key individual. The result appears to have been a huge win for all parties involved.

Helping People Realize Their Potential

Sometimes, there isn't a specific opportunity you can match with an individual's talents and career aspirations. In such cases, what you can do as an effective coach is to discern a strength, talent, or positive quality in your coachees that they themselves may not be fully aware of. This creates the opportunity to get them thinking about possibilities they may not have thought of before, potentially leading to a new career or even life-changing path.

A great example of this type of "elevating" comes from Best Coach Dr. Mark Brouker. He had a particularly memorable Elevate conversation with a direct report when he was a COO overseeing ten US Naval Hospitals.

Mark's direct report was a "really good doctor," very smart and accomplished. Moreover, he "had great leadership qualities, *though he didn't realize it.*" The leadership qualities Mark saw in this doctor included great listening skills, intelligence, tremendous ability as a clinician, and a genuine care for people.

> *At times, you need to consider the possibility that the best thing to do for your coachee is to help that person think about opportunities elsewhere – even if it means you may lose a valuable player on your team.*

Such a situation is ripe for an Elevate conversation during which a leader points out the potential in a direct report that the individual doesn't really see. Mark went on to explain that in the Navy you can stay in clinical practice or get on the Executive Medicine track, which leads to the C-suite of a hospital, possibly becoming a CEO or COO.

Given the potential Mark saw in this doctor as a candidate for the Executive Medicine track, the two of them had roughly a dozen conversations about this idea over the course of about two years. According to Mark, "A part of this ongoing dialogue was me helping him realize that he actually did have the natural leadership skills to be a CEO of a hospital, in addition to his intelligence and skills as a clinician." Mark added that one thing he said that seemed to persuade the doctor was, "If you don't pursue this, somebody else will, and they may not be as good as you would be."

Helping Someone Move Onward and Upward

People consistently tell us that the best coaches they have ever worked with truly care about them on a personal level. As Best Coach Alan Stein, professional coach to such elite athletes as NBA star Kevin Durant, puts it, "You must connect first and coach second." When we asked him to elaborate, he said, "Before you can coach someone, that person needs to know you really care about them as a person." At times, this means that you need to consider the possibility that the best thing to do for your coachee is to help that person think about opportunities elsewhere – even if it means you may lose a valuable player on your team.

A brief story from Best Coach Jessica Edwards, HR Manager at AMERISAFE, illustrates this idea. In a previous company, Jessica had an employee who, in her words, was "maxed out," meaning that no higher-level role would become available to her in that particular organization. Jessica empathized with the situation and understood that the message needed to be communicated in a delicate manner – providing clarity around the reality of the situation while also demonstrating care and support for the employee's continued success. So, Jessica let this individual know there was no logical next step for her within the organization, and she then supported her in finding the right opportunity elsewhere.

The high-potential, high-performing employee said she appreciated being candidly told what opportunities the company did and didn't have. What was the outcome? Jessica noted that the woman "ended up running the company" where she went.

The Elevate Matrix

A framework we like to use when we initiate this type of coaching conversation is what we call The Elevate Matrix (see Figure 11.1).

We first learned this tool, or at least an earlier version of it, from a consulting firm we have partnered with called Catalyst Change Consultants. The vertical axis in the matrix deals with how motivated a coachee is in different areas, and the horizontal axis deals with how skilled he or she is in different areas.

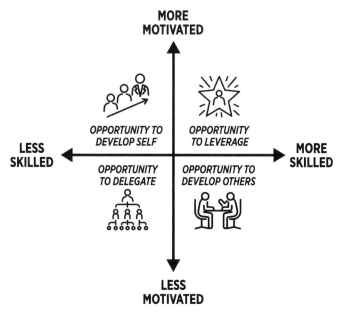

Figure 11.1 | *The Elevate Matrix*

We first ask a coachee to think about all the duties he or she has and to put each in one of the four quadrants in the matrix. For instance, the bottom left quadrant is for duties where the coachee is both relatively less skilled and less motivated to perform. If too much of someone's job falls into this quadrant, that person is probably in the wrong role and should look to make a career move! But everyone can generally identify something that falls into that quadrant. When possible, we think it's best to try to delegate such duties to others. All three coauthors, for example, have an administrative assistant who takes care of travel arrangements, expense reports, and so on (which are tasks that we admittedly are less motivated and perhaps a bit less skilled to accomplish when compared to the skills and strengths our assistants bring to the table).

The bottom right quadrant refers to duties the coachee is relatively more skilled at performing, but where the motivation level is still not especially high. These may even be areas where someone was at one point highly motivated, but where he or she, over time, simply got burned out on these particular duties. Where possible, we think this situation is a good opportunity to try to develop others so that a handoff can be made.

The upper left quadrant is for duties the coachee is actually quite motivated to perform but is less skilled at. The individual, then, may want to invest in getting some coaching or doing other developmental work. For instance, one of us recently had a coaching conversation with a member of our firm that focused on getting the coachee involved in training in an area he has a lot of interest in but no real education or experience to date.

The upper right quadrant represents areas in which the coachee is both highly skilled and highly motivated. In our view, duties that fall within this quadrant are opportunities for leverage. What we mean by the term "leverage" is simply that a good coach will help a coachee think through ways of using the skills that fit in this quadrant to the organization's or team's benefit, as well as to the coachee's own benefit.

To illustrate, one of us recently had a coaching conversation with a leader in one of our client organizations where the focus was on a position that was opening up in the organization. Completing the Elevate Matrix clearly showed that the coachee had lots of interest in the position – that is, he was motivated and, arguably, had the skills not only to step into the role but to excel in it. The coachee eventually got the role and, we believe, will be leveraging some skills in a new way, both to his benefit and to his firm's benefit.

In sum, the Elevate Matrix is a tool is designed for coaches to help coachees think about the overall range of things they are responsible for, unlike the other four types of coaching conversations that pertain to specific issues or current tasks or duties. We are increasingly using this matrix with our coaching clients with great results. The feedback we get is that it is a simple but powerful tool to help coachees think through things they should consider trying to delegate, areas where they could be developing others, areas where they should be developing themselves, and the key skills and interests they need to be effectively leveraging.

When to Have an Elevate Conversation

You should initiate an Elevate coaching conversation when the Coaching Cue of "accomplished" is present and the coachee's Central Issue is the need for growth and development. We would hope that at least some (if not many or most) of you reading this book find yourselves in that type of situation with the people you coach on a regular basis. After all, the result of effective coaching over time should be a team of people who are generally strong performers (in other words, "accomplished").

This would mean, of course, that the Elevate coaching conversation should be a common way to interact with at least some of the people you coach. Indeed, Best Coach Mary Watson told us, "I have this type of conversation with everyone I manage in our monthly one-on-one meetings."

Mary also alluded to another context in which the Elevate conversation is appropriate and important: When succession planning is being done. In other words, when it's time for deliberate thought to be put into bench strength (who is a viable replacement for whom, what are the ways in which people need to be developing in order to be candidates for certain more senior positions, and so on), having Elevate conversations with strong performers makes sense.

Yet another time to have this sort of conversation is, quite simply, when doing goal setting with strong performers. Encouraging them with regards to what they are already doing well and then challenging them with regards to what they can seek to accomplish next is a great way of keeping people feeling like they are growing and developing which, as we have noted, is a key driver of employee engagement.

Taking a Step Back

It's all too common for coaching conversations – for example, biweekly one-on-one meetings between a manager and a direct report – to focus primarily on specific tasks: "How is that project going? How can I help you with that deliverable?" And so on.

Yet, one of the primary goals our clients ask us to help them achieve is to make sure that their hi po employees are getting the feedback, coaching, and development they need in order to be engaged and retained. Consequently, we are increasingly counseling our clients to have their leaders periodically take a step back in their coaching conversations to say, essentially, "Let's set aside any discussion of the immediate tasks at hand for today." In place of the specifics, we encourage coaches to ask broader questions such as these:

- What are you really enjoying?
- How can we do more to ensure that we have you involved in things that really play to your strengths?
- In what areas are you eager to develop?
- What are some things you're doing that you think take you out of your sweet spot?
- What options might we explore for addressing any such situations?

A reasonable concern over initiating this sort of coaching conversation (at least, one that we sometimes hear from the leaders we work with) is: What if there really aren't a lot of opportunities for advancement in our organization? For example, one of us recently completed a workshop with a group of fairly senior leaders during which one person said, "We don't have a lot of turnover in this organization at our level and above, so it's not like there are lots of roles for people at the level below us to move into."

Our response to this legitimate question was twofold. First, keep in mind the distinction between "career development" (advancing in terms of position) and "professional development" (continuing to improve in terms of skills and abilities). We think people generally appreciate candid conversations with credible coaches regarding their potential for advancement within a given organization. And even if such opportunities are limited, people (including hi-po employees who, by nature, want to move up in their organization) still greatly value coaching and mentoring that helps them grow and develop in general – even if the chances of getting promoted in the near future are, in reality, somewhat limited.

Our second response concerns loyalty. We often meet people in our client organizations who say they worked for a given leader in one place, significantly grew and developed under that leader, moved to another employer – with that leader's full blessing and support – and then later went back to work for that leader again, either at the same company or at a different one. Sometimes this happens more than once. This sort of loyalty speaks volumes about the power you have as a coach seeking to "elevate" your people, even at the risk of losing them over the short term. As the saying goes, "What goes around comes around."

> ... *ask yourself:*
> *Am I doing enough to Elevate my people? What more could I do?*

In conclusion, we challenge you to ask yourself: Am I doing enough to Elevate my people? What more could I do? We hope this chapter provides good guidance on how to have this sort of conversation more often and more effectively.

The EVALUATE "Un-Coaching" Conversation

chapter
12

> *"When the student is ready, the teacher will appear."*
>
> ~ GAUTAMA BUDDHA – Monk, sage, philosopher, teacher and founder of Buddhism

CONGRATULATIONS! You're now well-versed in the importance of being adaptable as a coach, in the contextual factors that affect your success as a coach, in various cues from your coachees that you need to be aware of and respond to, and of course, in the Five Coaching Conversations. There is, however, one final type of conversation, so to speak, that we need to discuss – what we call the "Un-Coaching" Conversation, also referred to as the Evaluate conversation.

The reason for this admittedly awkward label is that the sort of evaluation we will discuss in this chapter may or may not actually be a coaching conversation, as such, or even a series of coaching conversations. Rather, the Evaluate aspect of a potential coaching situation involves weighing any information that helps you and/or other decision makers (perhaps even including the prospective coachee) think about and assess whether a coaching engagement or relationship is likely to be fruitful. An example from one of our coauthors illustrates how this can unfold.

Our coauthor's leadership and team development work with the senior management team of a small technology company had gone very well. There were signs that the work that the team was doing was having a positive impact on the organization's culture and climate. In fact, everybody involved – from the firm's president down to the middle-manager level – seemed to have bought into the work that was being done.

As an extension of that work, the organization's head of Human Resources suggested to the president that he would benefit from executive coaching. After some dialogue among the key players about the possibility of proceeding with the coaching, a decision was made not to do so. Ostensibly, the reason was that the organization was going through some significant changes and the timing just wasn't right. According to the head of HR, however, the "real" reason was that the president simply wasn't open to the feedback he might get as a part of a coaching engagement.

You'll recall from our lengthy discussion in Chapter 5, regarding a coachee's commitment, that one of the biggest predictors of improvement in a coaching relationship is the "ripeness" of the person to be coached.[61] Using the RIPEN acronym to evaluate the Coaching **Context** in this example, the leader seemed not to be "ripe" for coaching for one or more of these reasons:

- **REALIZATION.** He didn't realize or believe that he had one or more significant areas for development (and apparently didn't want to find out that he might)

---
[61] Gates, Graddy, and Lindekens, *How Leaders Improve*.

- **INCENTIVE.** He didn't see any upside for improving or downside for not improving
- **PRESSURE.** He didn't feel a sense of urgency to address any issues related to feedback he might receive
- **EXPECTATION.** He didn't believe that he actually could or would get better
- **NATURAL INCLINATION.** He was, perhaps, simply not the sort of person who is predisposed to this sort of self-development

So, rather than waste the leader's time and the firm's money, the company decided not to proceed with executive coaching. (As a postscript to this example, the technology company president has struggled in his role since the time of the decision to pass on coaching, but that's another story.) The key point here is that coaching should always involve some sort of evaluation. In this example, an up-front evaluation suggested that the context was such that proceeding with coaching was not justified.

Best Coach Marshall Goldsmith goes so far as to say that "the importance of the coach pales in comparison to the importance of the person being coached." Moreover, Marshall volunteered that if he is considering getting involved in an executive coaching engagement and determines that the coachee is not going to improve more than marginally, he will simply decline the engagement.

When asked how he differentiates between people who are likely to improve and those who aren't, Marshall cited three factors: 1) *courage* to receive feedback, which he says most people don't like to do; 2) *humility* to accept feedback and acknowledge things that one could be doing better; and 3) *discipline* to actually follow through on a process for improving. While not all coaches can simply walk away from a coaching engagement, the way Marshall is able to do as a very in-demand external executive coach, what all coaches *can* do is evaluate such factors as a given coachee's courage, humility, and discipline as part of the Coaching Context. The remainder of this chapter focuses on both *when* and *how* to do this sort of evaluation.

When to Evaluate

The Evaluate conversation can take place before, during, and/or after coaching. In the case of the technology company president, it happened beforehand and led to the decision not to proceed with coaching. In another real-world example, the Evaluate conversation happened on the back end of a months-long effort to coach Sonia, a leader one of us was working with who herself had been trying for months to coach a direct report with clear areas for development. While our coauthor did not have much of an opportunity to interact directly with the employee in question, Sonia consistently and credibly described her direct report as a disruptive force within the team who was insubordinate with her at times.

Sonia tried many different coaching approaches with the employee over the better part of a year. At times, she clearly explained what was expected of the employee, and she provided ongoing feedback about the employee's behavior and performance relative to these expectations. At other times, she explored options for how the employee could better address the issues she faced. At still other times, Sonia used combinations of positive feedback for healthy conduct and good performance along with explanations and, ultimately, the imposition of consequences of dysfunctional conduct and poor performance.

Yet, over time, nothing really seemed to change. Eventually, it became important to evaluate the situation and decide what the options were – options *other* than more coaching, which clearly wasn't doing the job. Because Sonia and Sonia's manager believed that they had given the employee every opportunity to essentially turn her situation around, and because the employee had not chosen to make any changes to her approach to work, the decision was made to let the employee go.

This example illustrates something that we have seen again and again over the course of our careers as management consultants. Whenever a team is experiencing significant dysfunction, it's almost invariably because at least one member of the team simply needs to be dismissed.

We are, of course, all for giving a struggling or even difficult employee every opportunity to turn things around through feedback, training, coaching, and the like. However, when dysfunction within the team is severe, it almost invariably seems to stem from "that person" who just fundamentally lacks the character to be able to change. He or she may be dishonest, manipulative, disrespectful, or exhibiting any number of other behaviors that are at the root of the team's dysfunction. At the risk of using an overly strong or sensitive analogy, this employee is often seen as a cancer within the team by many, most, or even all other team members.

Sometimes, cancer can be treated. But, very sadly, sometimes it can't. And, similarly, sometimes an honest evaluation of a troubled situation within a team or organization clearly reveals a person who can't or won't be helped with any amount of well-intentioned intervention.

These examples illustrate the Evaluate or "un-coaching" conversation – generally meaning a series of serious discussions that may lead to outcomes ranging from a decision not to proceed with coaching at a given point in time to the much more difficult but perhaps ultimately necessary decision to dismiss an employee.

Beyond such clear illustrations of up-front and back-end Evaluate conversations, we also believe that a part of any effective coaching effort that lasts for more than just one conversation should involve *periodic evaluation.* In other words, the coach (as well as the coachee and, potentially others, such as the coachee's manager if he or she is not also the coach) should be asking questions like, "Is the coachee demonstrating openness to feedback? Is he or she making behavior changes? Are any such changes having a positive impact?" In short, while there are clearly times to have a very specific Evaluate conversation before or after a coaching effort, there are other times when the effective coach will be responsible for ensuring that some sort of evaluation is happening every step of the way (as depicted in Figure 12.1).

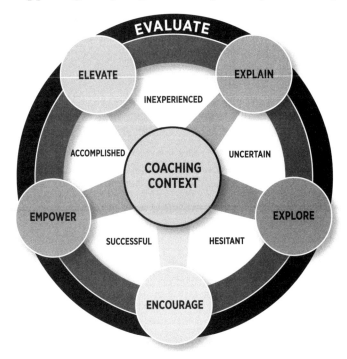

Figure 12.1 | *Evaluate- The "Un-Coaching" Conversation*

Again, an "Un-Coaching" Conversation might not be a conversation at all, and if it is a conversation (or more than one conversation), it might not really be the type of conversation that could be considered "coaching." Nonetheless, we think it is absolutely critical in any given situation to ask yourself the question, "Is this really a coaching situation?" Or, to put it more practically, "Is this a context that is conducive to a coach's efforts being effective?"

The RIPEN Assessment

While we believe that great coaches have the ability, whether innately or due to some combination of experience and knowledge, to effectively evaluate when a coachee is "ripe" for improvement, we also think it's helpful for coaches to have tools that can help with this very important aspect of a coaching engagement. So, we at Avion Consulting have developed an assessment called the RIPEN instrument to help coaches and others responsible for coaching decisions (such as leaders responsible for deciding whether to invest in coaching for a team member) evaluate a coachee's potential for improvement.

> *If you're interested in learning more about Avion's RIPEN assessment, you can visit https://surveys.avionconsulting.com/RIPEN*

The RIPEN instrument is a self-assessment, meaning that only the prospective coachee must complete it. The instrument asks questions about the coachee's ripeness for improvement in general (which, again, refers to the "natural inclination" for improvement), as well as his or her ripeness for improvement in a given area. After taking the assessment, the prospective coachee gets a detailed report indicating both a personal level of ripeness in general, as well as his or her level of ripeness with respect to each dimension in our RIPEN model (Realization, Incentive, Pressure, Expectation, and Natural Inclination).

We think this assessment is very valuable, in at least a couple of ways. First, it can help a coach, a coachee, and/or a coachee's sponsor (for example, his or her manager or employer) decide if investing time, energy, and money in a coaching engagement makes sense at a given point in time. Second, if a decision is made to proceed with a coaching engagement, it is very helpful to both the coach and the coachee to know the areas in which he or she is more and less ripe for improvement. Knowing this will, for example, help you emphasize areas in which a coachee may want to focus on becoming more "ripe" for improvement, rather than focusing exclusively on the specific action steps the coachee claims to be committed to taking.

For instance, if a coachee is low in terms of "incentive" to improve, rather than focusing on specific actions that may help the coachee get better in a given area, it may be more helpful for you and the coachee to have some dialogue with the coachee's manager to find out: What are the possible benefits to the coachee of improving, and/or the consequences of not improving?

To cite an actual example, one of us was involved in a coaching engagement with a senior leader in a world-renowned not-for-profit organization. This leader was very ambitious, and a key part of the coaching engagement was learning from his manager that he would not be advancing unless and until he addressed his Central

Issue, and that incentive helped the leader really focus on improving in that area. And we believe he did, in fact, get better over time.

How to Proceed

If you determine that someone isn't really ripe for development, the best course of action sometimes is to consider some sort of a job change within the organization (for instance, a move from an area where an individual is struggling to another area where he or she is more likely to be a good fit). In other cases, it becomes apparent – often after coaching has been attempted – that in order to "get an employee's attention" (and perhaps "ripen" the individual somewhat), the best course of action may be to put the person on some sort of "performance-improvement-plan," or PIP.

The reality, however, is that at times the best answer may be what WD-40 refers to as "inviting the employee to work for the competition." In fact, many of the companies we admire the most (including not only WD-40 but also Southwest Airlines, Zappos, and MGM Resorts, among others) are especially bold when it comes to letting employees go when they clearly aren't "coachable" or are in some way a misfit for the organization. These companies, and many other world-class organizations, make it a priority to treat people with respect and dignity when having this type of conversation with employees they have determined aren't going to work out.

But they likewise realize the wisdom behind the idea of "hiring slow and firing fast." In other words, they know how to have the Evaluate "Un-Coaching" Conversation early and often. Whether you are an external coach, an internal leader who seeks to coach your employees as effectively as possible, or an organizational decision maker who needs to determine when to invest in someone's development and when to, in essence, cut your losses, we believe the practice of evaluation before, during, and/or after coaching is a critical aspect of effective coaching.

Coaching and Team Development

chapter
13

> *"Coming together is a beginning, staying together is progress, and working together is success."*
>
> ~ HENRY FORD – Industrialist and business magnate

IN OUR TEAM DEVELOPMENT WORK WITH CLIENTS, we often suggest that several things have to happen in order for a leader to build a high-performing team. The key factors in the Avion Team-Building Model are *Selection, Retention, Engagement,* and *Development* – both at the individual and at the team level (Figure 13.1). And we believe that the best coaches personally excel at and set a great example with regards to each of these factors related to teambuilding. Let us briefly touch on each.

Selection

The great 2004 movie *Miracle* tells the story of the improbable and dramatic Gold Medal win by the United States Olympic Hockey team in 1980. One short scene nicely captures the essence of effective *selection* by a coach. Well before the tryout period has ended, the team's head coach, Herb Brooks, has already decided who he wants his players to be. When the executive director of the U.S.

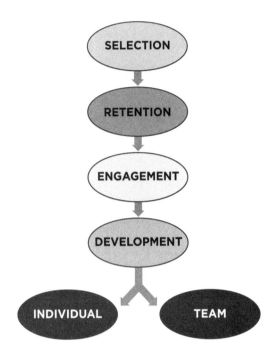

Figure 13.1 | *Avion Team-Building Model*

Olympic Committee sees the roster, he complains to Coach Brooks that he is leaving some of the "best players" off the team. Coach Brooks's response is classic: "I'm not looking for the *best* players," he replies, "I'm looking for the *right ones.*"

Coach Brooks realized what all great coaches know: There is much more to effective selection when putting a team together than just finding the people with the best possible technical skills. While a certain level of ability or aptitude is important in most team environments, of course, effective selection often has far more to do with nontechnical factors such as attitude, emotional intelligence, and coachability.

In his *Harvard Business Review* article "Hire for Attitude," Bill Taylor[62] cites several examples of organizations that "hire for attitude and

---
[62] Taylor, "Hire for Attitude."

train for skill," including the well-known corporate success story Southwest Airlines and other companies that use this strategy for selecting talent. The key idea is that an organization can train somebody to be able to perform the technical aspects of many jobs; on the other hand, it's difficult – if not impossible – to change the basic nature of an employee who has a fundamentally bad attitude!

In short, great coaches have a keen sense of what it takes to assemble a group of people capable of becoming a high-performing team. And this is true whether we are referring to a coach who is putting together a small team from scratch or an organization with thousands of employees that is seeking to ensure that the talent they are bringing on board always contributes to their high-performing culture.

Retention

Selecting the right people leads to the next step in building a high-performing team: *Retaining* the excellent talent that has joined the team. Some degree of organizational turnover is inevitable and healthy, of course. People retire; they leave due to changing personal circumstances; they move on to bigger and better opportunities, often with the full support of the organizations they are leaving; and occasionally it becomes clear that someone is simply a misfit for a given team for any of a number of reasons.

Yet, if a team or an organization is regularly losing strong talent – defined as people who are excellent performers with great attitudes and lots of "runway" (or potential) – that's clearly not a path to greatness. That's why one service our firm provides is designing, administering, and helping clients follow up on organizational surveys that, among other things, identify significant "drivers" (or "predictors") of what we call "intent to stay" – which is a measure related to talent retention.

The benefits of retaining good talent are numerous and critical: The organization is at less risk of losing valuable knowledge; constantly having to train new replacement employees can impact customer or client service; it's hard for a team to really get into a good rhythm if there is constant churn within the team; and it costs much more to hire a new employee than it does to retain an existing one. So, in light of these benefits, why is it that so many organizations struggle to retain good talent?

This question brings us to the relationship between good coaching and talent retention. When working with groups in our client organizations, we sometimes ask the question: Who has ever been in a situation where a great manager left an organization, and then soon after, numerous employees followed that great manager to his or her new company? Invariably, most hands go up.

Our follow-up question, of course, is: Why did these people follow these managers out the door? And the answers always seem to have to do with what we would identify with excellent coaching. "I felt like I was really being challenged and growing under that manager" or "This person really invested in me, both on a personal and on a professional level" are common sorts of responses. And these are things that, in our view, great coaches do.

Engagement

To put it another way, great coaches *engage* their people. Much has been written about the nature and importance of employee engagement over the last several years, and it can be defined in many ways. Based on work we have done in this area over the years with long-time collaborator Catherine Flavin-McDonald of Whole Leader, we think of "engagement" as having both a *heart* dimension and a *muscle* dimension.

The *heart* dimension refers to an employee's feelings about his or her team and/or organization. Does the employee feel a sense of loyalty? Challenge? Stimulation? Growth? Fun? The *muscle* dimension refers, essentially, to how much talent and energy the employee is willing to give to the job. Does he or she just do the bare minimum to get the job done, or does the employee go the proverbial extra mile? Does he or she get out of the office the moment the workday officially ends, or is the employee committed to doing what is necessary to get the job done right (within the parameters of what the law and a given company's policies allow for, naturally)?

Marcus Buckingham and Curt Coffman[63] popularized an intriguing idea: "People don't quit their jobs; they quit their bosses." We think there's a lot of truth to that, and we also think the inverse is true. People don't just feel engaged with regard to their jobs or companies; they feel engaged (or not) with regard to their managers.

In fact, over the years, we have designed and administered numerous employee engagement surveys, and as a part of this work, we always run a statistical procedure designed to identify the top predictors of overall employee engagement. At least two interesting findings generally emerge from this analysis.

First, if a given company has chosen to include survey items related to compensation, such items are, interestingly, almost never among the top drivers or predictors of employee engagement. That's not to say people are always happy with their compensation; quite

---
[63] Buckingham, Coffman, *First, Break All the Rules.*

the contrary. Yet it is utterly predictable that if a company includes compensation items in an employee engagement survey, they will be among the lower-rated survey items in terms of how satisfied people are with their pay. And this stands to reason – who would complete such a survey and essentially say, "I'm thrilled with my compensation; please don't pay me any more!"

But *"satisfaction with pay"* is a different question. The question we ask is not *how* satisfied people are with their pay, but rather whether satisfaction with pay is a significant driver or predictor of overall engagement. And it almost never is! Conversely, here's a survey item that is almost *always* a key predictor of overall engagement: "I feel I can grow and develop in my job."

In other words, based on the research we've done over the years, when employees feel like they are growing and developing in their jobs, they tend to be highly engaged. And who is largely responsible for that? The employee's manager! And how does a manager generally accomplish that outcome? By being a great coach!

Which leads us, incidentally, to the last element of our team performance framework. We have noted thus far that, in order to build a great team, it's necessary to *select* good talent, to *retain* that talent once on the team, and to keep your talent highly *engaged*. And a key to engagement is "growth and development"– both at the team and at the individual level.

Team Development

What does it mean to develop a team *as* a team? Suffice it to say that coaches who seek to develop an entire team effectively must make sure that they are skillfully guiding the team through several different but fairly predictable stages that groups pass through on the way to becoming high-performing teams.

But good coaches don't focus just on developing teams overall; they also focus on developing *individual players* on their teams. Put simply, if you are both helping a team "gel" together as a group and also helping each *individual* team member get better and better in terms of factors such as ability and motivation, you are on a path to seeing the team excel in terms of performance. Easier said than done, to be sure, but then, that's what much of this book has been about!

We have in mind by way of example a particular leader one of us has worked with who leads an extremely high performing "team" (actually, an entire organization) within his company. This leader has made it part of his mission to truly invest in the development of his team overall and of the individuals within his team. And, his is one of the highest-performing teams, based on hard business results, in his entire company. That's no coincidence. That's what great coaches do.

The Stages of Team Development

We noted in Chapter 2 that one of the models Avion Consulting uses when working with teams is the "Stages of Team Development" model originally developed by social psychologist Bruce Tuckman.[64] As many readers are likely aware, Tuckman noted that in order for a team in almost any context to reach the *Performing stage* (where challenging goals are being met), the team will almost certainly have to pass through three other stages: *Forming, Storming, and Norming.*

The Forming stage involves setting direction, clarifying roles and responsibilities, and the like. The Storming stage involves a more collaborative approach (think of "brainstorming") and requires

---

[64] Tuckman, "Developmental Sequence in Small Groups".

effective team conflict management. The Norming stage refers to a point at which a team has gotten into a positive flow regarding team member conduct, mutual accountability, and so on. And the Performing stage, as noted above, means the team is achieving challenging results at an outstanding level.

At some point, we also learned about a variation of Tuckman's model that added a fifth stage of team development called *Transforming*. We think this additional stage gets at an increasingly important organizational reality: Namely, that change is a constant in most contexts in which organizations operate, and that organizations that thrive are the ones which excel at continually transforming themselves through constant innovation and renewal. Leaders of such organizations eschew complacency and seek to constantly inspire people both to embrace change and to get better and better at finding and then executing on new and improved ways of doing what they do.

> *One way of conceiving of your role as a coach is to view it as taking the lead in moving a team through these stages of team development.*

One way of conceiving of your role as a coach is to view it as *taking the lead in moving a team through these stages of team development*. After all, the coach's job, first and foremost, is to maximize team performance . . . using whatever methods (within the range of what is legal, ethical, etc.) will accomplish that outcome. And, as you would expect, truly great coaches realize that they can't become complacent once they have helped a team or even an individual player achieve peak performance. There is always another coach who is finding a way to take his or her players to another level, so the best coaches have a "grow or die" mentality that sets them apart.

Interestingly, Tuckman's model, which has been so widely and so effectively used that its validity is essentially a truism, aligns perfectly with our Five Coaching Conversations model. Indeed, when that fifth stage – Transforming – is added, we believe that our model provides excellent direction regarding the coaching approach needed at each stage of team development in order to move a team to the next level.

"Forming" and the EXPLAIN Approach

When a team is forming, the Coaching Cue of *new* is present. In other words, the roles and responsibilities of each individual on the team may still be evolving, and the group as a whole is eager to understand how they fit within the bigger picture. In this stage of team development, it would benefit the team for you to use the Explain coaching approach by: Providing clear direction; outlining tasks, roles, and responsibilities; and providing quick and thorough responses to questions to ensure that the team has the guidance and level of specificity they need.

"Storming" and the EXPLORE Approach

In the storming stage of team development, the Coaching Cue of *uncertain* is present. A sense of competition, conflict, and high emotions arising within the group may be palpable as the members begin to push limits to establish group norms over time. Initiating an Explore coaching approach by asking powerful open-ended questions will help the team enter into an open dialogue. Their conversation will encourage the examination of possibilities and best practices around working together, as well as the exploration of different perspectives and ways of accomplishing tasks and addressing challenges as a cohesive team.

"Norming" and the ENCOURAGE Approach

Once the team has established group norms and experienced a sense of team cohesion, team members become engaged, their anxiety lessens, and they are ready to move forward and collaborate as a collective group. That said, the Coaching Cue of *hesitant* may still be present within the group. In other words, the members may be dealing with a lack of confidence in working together toward shared goals because they are doing so for the first time. This is an excellent opportunity to utilize the Encourage Coaching Conversation to recognize team efforts, celebrate successes, and provide valuable feedback to keep the team's energy and motivation high.

"Performing" and the EMPOWER Approach

Almost by definition, when a team has reached the "performing" stage, the Coaching Cue of *successful* is present. Once the team has demonstrated interdependence and has achieved *success* by producing as a team, it is time to provide team members with increased autonomy and to begin to lead from the sideline rather than from the front.

Leaders and coaches leveraging the Empower approach at this stage should be providing the team with pretty wide latitude to determine, or at least significantly influence, the way in which the team pursues its goals and objectives. In fact, we have noted that when we sit in on the meetings of high-performing teams, it's often hard to determine who the formal team leader is because team members have been empowered to such a degree that leadership is largely shared among them, regardless of position or formal authority.

"Transforming" and the ELEVATE Approach

In some cases, once a team has succeeded at whatever its mandate was, the team adjourns or disbands. This is generally the case for project teams and other types of groups that are pulled together solely to accomplish a specific goal. For example, consulting firms such as McKinsey & Company generally form "engagement teams" to work on specific client projects (sometimes called "studies"), and after a given study has been completed and presented to the client, the team disbands.

Often, however, teams are intended to stay together indefinitely, though the makeup of a team will change over time due to departures, additions, changes in leadership and other roles, and so on. Once this sort of team has performed at a high level over time, it can be said that it has moved beyond the Coaching Cue of *successful* to the Coaching Cue of *accomplished.*

In our experience, coaches of teams that are highly accomplished over time realize that one of their key responsibilities is to continue raising the bar by ensuring that the team never becomes complacent, that the team is continuously innovating, and that team members are being stretched and challenged.

In one team we have worked with, for example, the team leader's response to several consecutive years of great results and excellent retention among the strong performers on the team was to completely transform the team by making some fundamental changes to the team's operating model and changing people's roles so that they corresponded to the new model. The result was not only another year of strong performance but also increased engagement among certain team members who were challenged in new and exciting ways.

Putting It All Together

Recall the Coaching Cues we typed in italics throughout the discussion in this chapter: *New, Uncertain, Hesitant, Successful, Accomplished.* These Coaching Cues are present within the behaviors or actions of a group in each of the stages of team development in much the same way they present themselves within an individual coaching context. Paying attention to them allows you to gain additional insight to support the use of the most appropriate coaching conversation for the specific stage of development the team falls within.

Conclusion: Get Talking, Get Coaching

chapter **14**

"Knowing is not enough, we must apply. Willing is not enough; we must do."

~ BRUCE LEE – Actor, director, martial artist instructor, and philosopher

TOGETHER WE'VE WORKED OUR WAY THROUGH EACH OF THE FIVE COACHING CONVERSATIONS, as well as the "Un-coaching" Conversation — Evaluation. We've offered concepts to consider and tools to use when applying each of them, and we've shared stories with you from our interviewees, many of whom we consider Best Coaches and leaders across multiple industries – and many of whom have implemented one or more of the Five Coaching Conversations successfully. These leaders did not become excellent coaches overnight. They first had to understand their own strengths and development areas related to coaching, and then they had to commit (consciously or sub-consciously) to continuously improving over time. They did it, and so can you.

In this final chapter, we provide you with our recommendations and guidelines regarding how to apply the Five Coaching Conversations in several contexts. You'll recognize that the order of the three contexts parallels what we wrote in the introduction about who we had in mind as we developed our model and suggested practices. Namely:

- For the senior decision maker or influencer within an organization
- For the internal leader and/or coach who wants to use different diagnostics and coaching tools
- For the external coach who wants to expand and enhance his or her own practice

Let's look at each of these contexts in turn.

For the Organization

Perhaps you are a business owner, senior leader, or decision maker within an organization, and you'd like to implement a coaching practice within your organization. If so, we can offer you the following recommendations:

- Create a coaching and development strategy aligned to business goals.
- Create a culture that recognizes, supports, and celebrates both personal and professional development.
- Ensure that senior leaders and stakeholders actively support and are involved in the coaching process.
- Identify a cohort of internal and/or external coaches and involve them in the strategy for rolling out the coaching program.
- Ensure that coaches are aligned with the goals of the coaching program, models and methods used, etc.

- Consider rolling out a coaching skills assessment to internal coaches to assess their current skill. Follow up with education and practice to make sure that these coaches are able to leverage a variety of coaching tools and techniques in a way that resonates most with their coachees.

- Establish a cadence of check-ins with coaches and organization stakeholders to share insights and themes from coaching, and to ensure alignment of coaching best practices.

- Establish standards and/or create a template for individual development planning that can be utilized and tracked throughout the coaching engagement.

- Promote social learning, foster conversation and collaboration, and promote an environment where coachees across the organization are accountable and responsible for their own personal learning. This can be achieved by establishing a cadence in which coachees interact with and learn from each other by sharing action plans/development plans, as well as knowledge and insights from coaching.

- Track ROI and progress on individual development by establishing a process that evaluates baseline expectations and development objectives with post-coaching-program outcomes for individual coaching.

For the Internal Leader and Coach

Internal leaders and coaches can leverage the concepts, tools, and methodology of the Five Coaching Conversations with those they lead and support in the following ways:

- As a diagnostic and/or coaching tool with their direct reports or the team they lead.

- As a conversation tool with peers to aid in establishing credibility, rapport, and trust.
- As a set of coaching best practices to share with other leaders and coaches as a way of establishing an internal coaching practice and/or coaching center of excellence.
- As a self-diagnostic tool for level-setting and expanding upon current coaching skills.
- Utilizing multiple aspects of the Five Coaching Conversations framework to support common human resources and organizational talent development initiatives, including:
  - Leveraging the Explain Coaching Conversation as a process to facilitate both constructive and positive feedback related to performance management conversations.
  - Leveraging the Explore Coaching Conversation framework to integrate an open-ended, experience and behavior-based questioning approach during the interviewing and hiring process.
  - Using the Encourage Coaching Conversation as a framework to address complacency, noncompliance, and low performance by assessing and leveraging individual motivators.
  - Leveraging the Empower and Elevate Coaching Conversations as tools to build bench strength, as well as to assist in the succession planning process.
  - Using the model as a diagnostic tool for level-setting current skill level to ensure that new hire training programs are able to flex to accommodate the skills and aptitude of each program participant.

- Using the model as a diagnostic tool to provide a holistic approach to the individual development planning process and to ensure that the level of training, development, guidance, and support provided matches the individual's needs.

- Using the framework as a way to assess and grow coaching ability in other leaders. For example, if you're hiring people who will be leading others, promoting someone into a leader position, or implementing coaching skills practice with leaders across the board in an effort to "sharpen the saw" in this area and establish a consistent internal coaching practice, assess their current coaching skills and aptitude based on the Five Coaching Conversations model and integrate results into an ongoing development plan.

- Leveraging coaching context and cues as a diagnostic tool to determine what types of individual development and/or stretch assignments are needed for specific tasks. If a coachee continues to demonstrate similar coaching cues for a specific task, you can match the appropriate level of support to the coachee for that task. Take, for example, newness and/or uncertainty, which are two common Coaching Cues for the Explain Coaching Conversation. If the coachee continues to demonstrate these two cues around a specific task, it can suggest that providing more formal training on the task would be beneficial. If the coachee has demonstrated multiple successes over time and is therefore considered "accomplished" (an Elevate Coaching Conversation cue) in a certain task, it can suggest that the coachee is ready to take on a more complex task as well as become a mentor for those who are new to the task.

The key to unlocking these recommendations is for you to step back and look at the coachee as a whole person and realize that anyone, at any given time, can be successful or accomplished in one task or one area of responsibility and also be uncertain or unmotivated or hesitant in a different task or area of responsibility. Are you able to gather this input and then adapt your coaching approach to the person based on the context and nuance of the coaching conversation?

Additionally, as people settle into their roles over time and achieve a certain level of success, they become comfortable. When people are a bit too comfortable, they don't necessarily take the initiative to stretch and grow. The Five Coaching Conversations can be a helpful model to nudge people to think about the possibilities and options available to them regarding what's next for them in their roles, in their careers, etc. This nudge can help coachees step outside their comfort zone and into their greatness, to access and leverage their strengths, and to identify and fine-tune areas for development in a way that maximizes the impact they can have in their current and future roles.

For the External Coach

Many of the recommendations listed for the internal leader and coach can also be useful for the external coach; however, we would like to outline some additional recommendations specific to the external coach role in this section.

Whether they are new to coaching or more familiar and tenured in coaching expertise, external coaches can leverage the concepts, tools, and methodology of the Five Coaching Conversations to tune up their coaching game in the following ways:

- Utilize the Five Coaching Conversations framework to gain a holistic approach and process to coaching that weaves in multiple coaching frameworks, therefore expanding your skill set versus limiting yourself to one or two of your favorite go-to models.

- Establish (additional) credibility with your clients by having the flexibility of a multidimensional coaching model that leverages conversations and tools that can be matched with the coachee's current level of ability and motivation around a specific issue.

- Assess your own coaching expertise and identify which types of coaching conversations are your current go-to's and which are more unfamiliar. Grow and stretch yourself to increase competence across all coaching conversations so you can provide a balanced coaching approach with your clients.

- Organize your thoughts by gathering cues and context around the data you're receiving from your coaching clients and provide a framework to assist you in articulating your thoughts, insights, and guidance back to the client in an organized and meaningful way.

- Help the leaders you coach develop others by educating them about specific coaching tools they can use as activities with those they lead and support.

A note for new coaches:

The Five Coaching Conversations model provides a road map to help you navigate the overall coaching journey. It includes structured ways to analyze and report data gathered during a coaching interaction and align them with the coaching conversation that will resonate most with a coaching client.

> **A note for the more tenured coach:**
>
> Sometimes we need to make sure that we don't get too comfortable. Take time for ongoing self-reflection about your coaching ability. Ask yourself such thought-provoking questions as these:
>
> Do you know which types of coaching conversations you gravitate toward and which you avoid?
>
> What is the impact to your coaching clients when you avoid certain types of coaching conversations?
>
> What is the benefit of establishing a more balanced approach?

We have decades of collective experience as external coaches, and if there's one thing we've learned along the way that we would like to pass on with regard to "sharpening the coaching skills saw," it's that anyone must first understand how to do it, then do it, and then do it well. Understand that there's a difference here. Practically speaking, knowing how to navigate each of the Five Coaching Conversations is one thing, but if you want to be a great coach, the key is to learn how to do it artfully and in a way that resonates with your clients. The only way to accomplish this is through active practice and self-reflection. Practice makes progress, progress is impossible without change, and if something doesn't challenge you, it won't change you.

The Coaching Conversations Assessment

Thank you, dear reader, for adding our book to your library. We hope you have gained insight into the way you can use the Five Coaching Conversations model within your organization, with your team, and in your coaching practice. There is one more way in which the model can be utilized, and this one is centered around YOU. In order to improve, in order to change, whether your intention is self- or others-focused, you have to start somewhere. In our collective experience and research, for our most improved leaders, this change "begins within," with a sense of personal accountability and responsibility to make a positive impact.

Our Coaching Conversations Assessment provides you with a jump start on assessing your current coaching aptitude. Your results will provide an overview of your most and least preferred coaching approaches, along with personalized application tips so you can take the next step in becoming more comfortable with and skilled at having each of the five coaching conversations.

If you want to know more about utilizing the Five Coaching Conversations model, you can visit us at

www.fivecoachingconversations.com

Or, if you want to take our
Coaching Conversations Assessment, you can visit
https://surveys.avionconsulting.com/CCA

Keeping It Real

In *How Leaders Improve,* the authors speak to ten specific research-based insights that enable leaders to improve. One of these insights is the ability to "keep it real" with yourself, and with others.[65]

What do we mean by keeping it real? Consider the power that comes from hearing a leader acknowledge to others that he or she has room for improvement. Not only does this demonstrate

---

[65] Gates, Graddy, and Lindekens, How Leaders Improve, 145.

self-awareness and humility, it probably inspires others to be more open about their own development too. In addition, we believe it simultaneously communicates a sense that is it OK to be imperfect while also creating an expectation that everyone should strive to improve over the course of time.

The research behind *How Leaders Improve* revealed that the most improved leaders demonstrated this balance of self-awareness and humility by authentically sharing their strengths and their development areas with others. There was more to it than that, though. These leaders remained authentic to themselves as well; they remained committed and personally accountable to their own development over time. This mental and behavioral authenticity is what we call "keeping it real."

Figure 14.1 | *Keeping it Real*

You can keep it real with the Five Coaching Conversations by paying attention to the following four aspects of authenticity (see Figure 14.1):

- **SELF-AWARENESS:** Be honest with yourself concerning your current coaching skills and aptitude. Ask and answer candidly such questions as: What are my strengths, and where can I improve? What facts, data, assessment results, experience, and feedback can I pull from to gain insight into these areas?

- **COMMITMENT TO SELF-IMPROVEMENT:** Given the awareness you have gathered about your current coaching skills and aptitude, what action(s) are you committed to taking? How will you know you have succeeded in your efforts?

- **TRANSPARENCY AND FOLLOWING UP WITH OTHERS:** Who is supportive of your development and will help keep you accountable for your actions and commitments? Do you have an accountability buddy who is on a similar journey of development? Can you identify and work with a mentor whose strengths mirror the areas in which you aspire to develop? Share your personal insights and commitments with these people and agree upon a follow-up cadence to stay connected.

In summary, the Five Coaching Conversations model provides a holistic view of coaching as a journey that requires various types of conversations and tools for you to leverage in a way that resonates most with the coachee in a given Coaching Context. The model can be used as a self-diagnostic tool by leaders and coaches wishing to sharpen their coaching skills; it can be applied by leaders and coaches with those they coach and support; and it can be utilized as a structure and process in support of organizational initiatives. The outcome of each of these uses of the model is similar and echoes what we touched on in the very beginning of this book: Coaching at its most basic level should help people develop their potential in order to maximize performance in one or more areas.

We wish you the best in your coaching journey and look forward to sharing additional insights and research with you!

> *"Coaching is an interaction between two or more people, led by someone with content expertise and/or process skill, for the purpose of maximizing the performance and development of the coachee(s)."*
>
> ~ AVION CONSULTING

Bibliography

Alexander, Graham. "Behavioural Coaching—The GROW Model." *In Excellence in Coaching: The Industry Guide.* 2nd ed. edited by Jonathan Passmore, 83-93. Philadelphia: Kogan Page, 2010. First published by Kogan Page (London) 2006.

Ben-Shahar, Tal, and Angus Ridgway. *The Joy of Leadership: How Positive Psychology Can Maximize Your Impact (and Make You Happier) in a Challenging World.* Hoboken, NJ: Wiley, 2017.

Blanchard, Kenneth H., and Garry Ridge. *Helping People Win at Work: A Business Philosophy Called "Don't Mark My Paper, Help Me Get an A."* Upper Saddle River, NJ: Pearson Education, 2009.

Bradberry, Travis, and Jean Greaves. *Emotional Intelligence 2.0: Mastery Your Emotions, Develop and Boost Your EQ to Improve the skill to Business and Relationship.* San Diego, CA: TalentSmart, 2009.

Buckingham, Marcus, and Curt Coffman. *First, Break All the Rules: What the World's Greatest Managers Do Differently.* New York: Simon & Schuster, 1999.

Burns, James MacGregor. *Leadership.* New York: Harper Perennial Modern Classics, 2010. First published by Harper & Row 1978.

Covey, Stephen R. *The 7 Habits of Highly Effective People.* New York: Free Press, 1989.

de Vries, Manfred Kets, and Elisabet Engellau. "A Clinical Approach to the Dynamics of Leadership and Executive Development." *In Handbook of Leadership Theory and Practice*, edited by Nitin Nohria and Rakesh Khurana. Boston, MA: Harvard Business Press, 2010.

Dweck, Carol. Mindset: *The New Psychology of Success.* Random House, 2006.

Fazio, Rob. *Simple Is the New Smart: 26 Success Strategies to Build Confidence, Inspire Yourself, and Reach Your Ultimate Potential.* Wayne, NJ: Career Press, 2016.

Fine, Alan, and Rebecca R. Merrill. *You Already Know How to Be Great: A Simple Way to Remove Interference and Unlock Your Greatest Potential.* New York: Penguin, 2010.

Gardner, Howard. *Frames of Mind: The Theory of Multiple Intelligences.* 3rd ed. New York: Basic Books, 2011. First published by Basic Books 1983.

Gallup, Inc. "State of the American Manager." Gallup.com. https://www.gallup.com/services/182138/state-american-manager.aspx.

Garvin, David A. "How Google Sold Its Engineers on Management." Harvard Business Review, December 2013, https://hbr.org/2013/12/how-google-sold-its-engineers-on-management.

Gates, John, Jeff Graddy, and Sacha Lindekens. *How Leaders Improve: A Playbook for Leaders Who Want to Get Better Now.* Santa Barbara, CA: Praeger, 2017.

Goldsmith, Marshall, and Mark Reiter. *What Got You Here Won't Get You There: How Successful People Become Even More Successful!* New York: Hyperion, 2007.

Goleman, Daniel. *Emotional Intelligence: Why It Can Matter More Than IQ.* New York: Bantam, 1995.

Goleman, Daniel. *Working with Emotional Intelligence.* New York: Bantam, 1998.

Gottman, John, and Nan Silver. *The Seven Principles for Making Marriage Work.* Harmony Books, 2000.

Graddy, Jeff, and Sacha Lindekens. *Ready, Set, RIPEN! A Leader's Guide to Preparing People for Development.* San Diego, CA: Avion Consulting, 2019.

Hersey, Paul, Kenneth H. Blanchard, and Dewey E. Johnson. *Management of Organizational Behavior: Leading Human Resources.* Upper Saddle River, NJ: Prentice-Hall, 1969.

Hendrickson, Robert. *The Facts on File Encyclopedia of Word and Phrase Origins.* New York: Checkmark Books, 2000.

Herzberg, Fredrick. *The Motivation to Work.* New York: John Wiley & Sons, 1959.

Hill, Linda A. "Becoming the Boss." *Harvard Business Review,* January 2007, https://hbr.org/2007/01/becoming-the-boss.

Katzenbach, Jon. "The Steve Jobs Way." Strategy + Business, May 29, 2012, https://www.strategy-business.com/article/00109.

Keirsey, David, and Marilyn Bates. *Please Understand Me: Character and Temperament Types.* 5th ed. Carlsbad, CA: Prometheus Nemesis Book Company, 1984.

Kouzes, James M., and Barry Z. Posner. *Credibility: How Leaders Gain and Lose It, Why People Demand It.* 2nd ed. San Francisco: Jossey-Bass, 2011.

Landsberg, Max. *The Tao of Coaching: Boost Your Effectiveness at Work by Inspiring and Developing Those around You.* London: Profile Books, 2015. First published by HarperCollins 1996.

Larson, Carylynn. "Coaching Isn't Just Asking Questions." *Forbes,* November 21, 2018, https://www.forbes.com/sites/forbescoachescouncil/2018/11/21/coaching-isnt-just-questions/#74761e9c47a1.

Lewin, Kurt, Ronald Lippitt, and Ralph K. White. "Patterns of Aggressive Behavior in Experimentally Created 'Social Climates.'" *Journal of Social Psychology* 10, no. 2 (1939): 269-299. doi:10.1080/00224545.1939.9713366.

Losada, Marcial, and Emily Heaphy. "The Role of Positivity and Connectivity in the Performance of Business Teams: A Nonlinear Dynamics Model." *American Behavioral Scientist* 47, no. 6 (February 2004): 740-755. doi:10.1177%2F0002764203260208.

Maslow, Abraham. "A Theory of Human Motivation." *Psychological Review* 50, no. 4 (1943): 370-396. doi:10.1037/h0054346.

McCrae, Robert R., and Paul T. Jr. Costa. *Personality in Adulthood.* 2nd ed. New York: GuilfordPress, 2003.

McNeely, Madeline, and Michelle Ehrenreich. "How to Adopt a Coaching Mentality and Practice." Harvard Extension School: Professional Development, January 16, 2019. https://www.extension.harvard.edu/professional-development/blog/how-adopt-coaching-mentality-and-practice.

Milner, Julia, and Trenton Milner. "Most Managers Don't Know How to Coach People. But They Can Learn." *Harvard Business Review,* August 14, 2018. https://hbr.org/2018/08/most-managers-dont-know-how-to-coach-people-but-they-can-learn.

Merrill, David W., and Roger H. Reid. *Personal Styles and Effective Performance.* Boca Raton, FL: CRC Press, 1981.

Moen, F. and Skaalvik, E. . "The Effect from Executive Coaching on Performance Psychology." *International Journal of Evidence Based Coaching and Mentoring* 7 no. 2(2009): 31-49. https://radar.brookes.ac.uk/radar/items/89e11575-fa06-473a-a6ab-8d202ca4e5d0/1/.

Myers, Isabel Briggs, and Mary H. McCaulley. *Manual: A Guide to the Development and Use of the Myers-Briggs Type Indicator.* Palo Alto: Consulting Psychologists Press, 1985.

Pascotto, Valerio. "Why Coaching Is A Necessary Leadership Style In A Matrix Organization." *Forbes,* May 23, 2019. https://www.forbes.com/sites/forbescoachescouncil/2019/05/23/why-coaching-is-a-necessary-leadership-style-in-a-matrix-organization/#135219a64e33.

Passmore, Jonathan. "An Integrative Model for Executive Coaching." *Consulting Psychology Journal: Practice and Research* 59, no. 1 (March 2007): 68-78. doi:10.1037/1065-9293.59.1.68.

Patterson, Kerry, Joseph Grenny, Ron McMillan, and Al Switzler. *Crucial Conversations: Tools for Talking When Stakes Are High.* 2nd ed. New York: McGraw-Hill, 2012.

Pink, Daniel H. *Drive: The Surprising Truth about What Motivates Us.* New York: Riverhead Books, 2009.

Scouts BSA. *The First Edition 1911.* Minneola, NY: Dover Publications, 2005.

Seligman, Martin. "PERMA and the Building Blocks of Well-Being." *The Journal of Positive Psychology* 13, no. 4 (February 2018): 333–35. doi:10.1080/17439760.2018.1437466.

Seppala, Emma and Kim Cameron. "Proof That Positive Work Cultures Are More Productive." *Harvard Business Review,* December 1, 2015. https://hbr.org/2015/12/proof-that-positive-work-cultures-are-more-productive.

Sinek, Simon. *Start with Why: How Great Leaders Inspire Everyone to Take Action.* New York: Portfolio/Penguin, 2009.

Taylor, Bill. "Hire for Attitude, Train for Skill." *Harvard Business Review,* February 1, 2011. https://hbr.org/2011/02/hire-for-attitude-train-for-sk.

Theeboom, Tim, Bianca Beersma, and Annelies E.M. Van Vianen. "Does Coaching Work? A Meta-analysis on the Effects of Coaching on Individual Level Outcomes in an Organizational Context." *The Journal of Positive Psychology* 9, no. 1 (2013): 1-18. doi:10.1080/17439760.2013.837499.

Tuckman, Bruce W. "Developmental Sequence in Small Groups." *Psychological Bulletin* 63, no. 6 (1965): 384-99.

Weitzel, Sloan R. *Feedback That Works: How to Build and Deliver Your Message.* Greensboro, NC: Center for Creative Leadership, 2000.

Whitmore, John. *Coaching for Performance.* 5th ed. London: Nicholas Brealey, 2017. First published by Nicholas Brealey 1992.

Zenger, John H., and Kathleen Stinnett. *The Extraordinary Coach: How the Best Leaders Help Others Grow.* New York: McGraw-Hill, 2010.

Zenger, Jack, and Joseph Folkman. "The Ideal Praise-to-Criticism Ratio." *Harvard Business Review,* March 15, 2013. https://hbr.org/2013/03/the-ideal-praise-to-criticism.html.

Zheng, Xingshan, Ismael Diaz, Yin Jing, and Dan S. Chiaburu. "Positive and Negative Supervisor Developmental Feedback and Task-Performance." *Leadership & Organization Development Journal* 36, no. 2 (April 2015): 212–32. doi:10.1108/lodj-04-2013-0039.

About the Authors

John Gates, Ph.D.

John is a Partner with Avion Consulting. He provides coaching and counsel to leaders from the middle management to senior executive levels; he partners with clients in the design and implementation of high-impact leadership development solutions; and he works with management teams on issues related to both team and organizational effectiveness. He is also a coauthor of Avion Consulting's previously released book *How Leaders Improve: A Playbook for Leaders Who Want to Get Better Now*, an Amazon #1 new release.

John began his career in higher education and has served in both faculty and leadership positions at several universities.

John has a Ph.D. in Organizational Communication from the University of Southern California.

Morgan Massie, M.A.

Morgan is a Consultant with Avion Consulting. She provides organizations with talent strategies that are focused on elevating and retaining individuals, empowering and engaging teams, and partnering with clients in the design, development, and implementation of award-winning leadership development initiatives.

Morgan began her career in psychology before transitioning into the field of corporate organization and talent development in which she held multiple internal management and senior management roles prior to transitioning into the field of leadership consulting and coaching. She has experience across a variety of industries and holds professional certifications in human resources, learning program design and facilitation, lean/six sigma, and leadership consulting and coaching.

Morgan has a B.A. in Psychology from the University of South Florida, a M.A. in Instructional Systems Design from the University of Central Florida, and a certification in Positive Psychology and Resilience from the University of Pennsylvania.

Steve Williams, M.A.

Steve is a Partner with Avion Consulting. He demonstrates skill at analyzing and leveraging qualitative and quantitative data, and then makes bottom-line observations and recommendations to challenge and support effective decision-making. Steve has partnered with clients for more than twenty years to find impactful and practical solutions to real business issues.

Steve began his career in human resources, advancing into HR leadership positions before subsequently going into external consulting several years later.

Steve has a B.A. and an M.A. in the behavioral sciences and has studied leadership at the doctoral level at the University of San Diego.

About Avion

Avion Consulting partners with senior leaders and their organizations to unleash potential in people. We contribute to our clients' success by providing tailored solutions that positively impact people and drive business results. Our leadership development professionals bring unique experiences and skills to our work with clients, but one thing we all have in common is a deep commitment to helping leaders and organizations achieve their full potential.

Avion consultants have spent decades serving premier clients across the globe. We believe our experience, our expertise, and our commitment to integrity and excellence make the difference for our clients. Be sure to ask any of us where the name Avion Consulting came from; we will be more than happy to tell you the story.

Index

NOTE: Page references in ***bold italics*** refer to figures.

A

Ability, performance and, 64–66, 143–144
Accomplished cue, ***86***, 90–91, 222
Active listening, 84–85
Adams, John, 33
Adaptability, 21–32
    in action, 29–30
    emotional intelligence of coachee and, 27–30
    leadership style of coachee and, 23–27
    maximizing performance and growth through, 21
    mindset and skillset for, 21–22
    personality of coachee and, 22–23
    understanding Coaching Context for, 30–32, 34
    Advice, offering, 96–102, ***98***
Albertson, Darryl, 109, 156–157, 176–177, 189, 190–191
Alexander, Graham, 10¬
Angelou, Maya, 143
Appreciation, expressing, 150–154
Asad, Hina, 88, 137, 177, 179
Attention-getting approaches, 160–161
Authenticity, 231–234, ***232***
Autonomy, motivation and, 145–146, 169–170, 174
Avion Consulting. *See also* Five Coaching Conversations model; ISEE (Issue, Situation, Exploration, Execution) model
    contact information, 207, 231

Credibility model of, 59, **60**
How Leaders Improve (Gates, Graddy, and Lindekens), 33–34, 66–67, 121, 184, 231–232
Learning Bridge partnership of, 36–37
mission statement of, 9

B
"Becoming the Boss" (Hill), 59
Ben-Shahar, Tal, 146
Best Coaches, defined, 35–42
Big Five (personality) model, 22
Blanchard, Ken, 24–27, 65, 93
Bochy, Bruce
    attention-getting approach of, 161
    Best Coach designation of, 39
    on empowerment, 175, 183
    on motivation, 150
Boy Scouts of America, 115
Bradberry, Travis, 27–28
Brashears, Liz
    Best Coach designation of, 39
    on coaching cues, 91–92
Brooks, Herb, 211–212
Brouker, Mark
    on appreciation, 152–155
    Best Coach designation of, 39
    on elevating coachee, 192
    on empowerment, 183
    on Explain Coaching Conversation, 128–129
    on offering advice, 100–101
Buckingham, Marcus, 215
Burns, James MacGregor, 24

C

Cameron, Kim, 146–147
Center for Audit Quality, 79–80
Center for Creative Leadership, 111–113
Central Issue
  Encourage Coaching Conversation and, 165
  focus as, 54–56, **55**
  ISEE model and, 121–122, 132–134
Character, 62–63
Coachee(s). *See also* Coaching Context; Five Coaching Conversations model
  adaptability of coaching style for, 21–32
  Commitment of, 66–72
  Competence of, 64–66, 131
  Confidence of, 72–73, 131
  defined, 45
Coaching, xv–xvii. *See also* Adaptability; Coaching Context; Coaching cues; Five Coaching Conversations model; Question-asking paradigm of coaching
  coach, origin of term, 50–51
  coach-as-surrogate problem, 114
  "coaching upward," 137–138
  Credibility of coach, 57–63, **60,** 130
  defined, 44–46
  effectiveness of, xv–xvi
  for performance and potential, 3–6
  research on, xvi–xvii
Coaching Context, 57–80
  adapting to, 30–32, 34 (*See also* Adaptability)
  Commitment of coachee, 66–72
  Competence of coachee, 64–66, 131
  Confidence of coachee, 72–73
  Context Cone of, 73–75, **74, 75**
  Credibility of coach, 57–63, **60,** 127, 130
  Criticality of issue, 63–64, 131

for effective coaching, 57–58
for Encourage Coaching Conversation, 147–148
for Explain Coaching Conversation, 100, 108, 109, 116–117
as hub of coaching wheel, **76,** 76–77
judgment used with, 77–80, **79**
sports *vs.* organizational context, 1–3, 46–48
Coaching Cues, 81–92
active listening for, 84–85
building personal list of cues, 91–92
case study, 82–85
Coaching Wheel, forward and backward, **85**
matching cues to conversations, 85–91, **86,** 134–135
for team development, 222
transitioning between Coaching Conversations, 81–82
Coaching Index survey items (Leadership Inventory, Learning Bridge), 36–38, 53, 54
"Coaching Isn't Just Asking Questions" (Larson), 15
Coaching Wheel. *See also* Coaching Context
active listening with, 84–85
building personal list of cues for, 91–92
Coaching Context as hub of, **76,** 76–77
forward and backward, **85**
matching cues to conversations, 85–91, **86**
overview, **52,** 52–54, **53**
term for, 50–51
transitioning between Coaching Conversations, 81–85
Coffman, Curt, 215
Cole, Matt, 107, 113–115, 126–127, 140–141, 166
Commitment
of coachee, 66–72
Context Cone and, 73–75, **74, 75**
to self-improvement, 232, 233
Competence
of coach, 60–62
of coachee, 64–66, 131
Context Cone and, 73–75, **74, 75**

Confidence. *See also* Coaching Context
   of coachee, 72–73, 131
     Context Cone and, 73–75, **74, 75**
     as key to Coaching Context, 80
Consequences, clarifying, 158–159
Context Cone, 73–75, **74, 75**
Costa, Paul, 22
Covey, Stephen, 63, 149
Credibility
   Avion model of, 59, **60**
   character and, 62–63
   Competence and, 60–62
   Credibility: How Leaders Gain and Lose It, Why People Demand It (Kouzes and Posner), 59
   defined, 58–59
   ISEE model and, 127
   The Office (TV show) example, 58
Criticality of issue
   Context Cone and, 74
   defined, 63–64
   ISEE model and, 131
Crucial Conversations (Patterson), 114
Cues. See Coaching cues

D

Decision making, judgment for, 77–80, **79**
De Nicola, Tony, Best Coach designation of, 39
Development of teams. See Team development
Direction, giving, **98**, 108–110
DiTondo, Michelle
   Best Coach designation of, 39
   on confidence, 157
   on stating expectations, 104
Drive (Pink), 169
Durant, Kevin, 40, 193
Dweck, Carol, 160

E

EDGE (Explain, Demonstrate, Guide, Enable) method, 115–116
Edwards, Jessica, 88–89, 193
Ehrenreich, Michelle, 5
Elevate Coaching Conversation, 185–199
    Coaching Wheel, overview, 51–54, **52, 53**
    Context Cone and, 73–75, **74, 75**
    The Elevate Matrix for, 193–196, **195**
    goal of, 185–188
    for high-potential, high-performing (hi-po) employees, 188–189
    initiating, 196–197
    ISEE model for, 188
    loyalty and, 199
    matching Accomplished cue to, **86,** 90–91
    matching skills with opportunities for, 190–191
    overview, 43–44
    personal interest in coachee for, 193
    professional development *vs.* career development and, 198
    for realizing potential, 191–192
    Situational Leadership for, 188
    taking step back for, 197–198
    transforming and team development, 221–222
    understanding goals and aspirations for, 189–190
Emotional intelligence, 27–30
Empower Coaching Conversation, 169–184
    as active process, 172
    challenge of, 183–184
    Coaching Wheel, overview, 51–54, **52, 53**
    Context Cone and, 73–75, **74, 75**
    goal of, 169–170
    initiating, 182–183
    matching Successful cue to, **86,** 89–90
    overview, 43–44
    performing and team development, 220

problems of, 170–172
questions to ask for, 173–182, 182
Encourage Coaching Conversation
    attention-getting approaches to, 160–161
    celebrating successes with, 157–158
    clarifying incentives and consequences with, 158–159
    Coaching Context of, 147–148
    Coaching Wheel, overview, 51–54, **52, 53**
    Context Cone and, 73–75, **74, 75**
    explaining the "why" with, 154–155
    expressing appreciation in, 150–154
    goal of, 143–144
    initiating, 162–165
    instilling confidence with, 155–157
    matching Hesitant cue to, **86,** 87–89
    motivation and, 143–146
    norming and team development, 220
    overview, 43–44
    Positive Psychology for, 146–147
    as safety net, 159–160
    Strengths-Based Development for, 147
    trust and, 165–167
    understanding and, 148–150
Engagement (team development), 211, **212,** 214–217
Evaluate "Un-Coaching" Conversation, 201–210
    for assessing coaching relationship, 201–202
    how to proceed if person isn't "coachable," 209–210
    RIPEN tool for, 202–204, 207–209
    timing of, 204–207, **206**
Expectation(s)
    Confidence of coachee and, 72–73
    RIPEN tool, 67–72, 202–204, 207–209
    stating, **98,** 104–106
Experience (expertise), sharing, **98,** 106–108
Explain Coaching Conversation, 93–117

252 FIVE COACHING CONVERSATIONS

    avoiding problems with, 94–95
    Coaching Wheel, overview, 51–54, **52, 53**
    Context Cone and, 73–75, **74, 75**
    EDGE (Explain, Demonstrate, Guide, Enable) method for, 115–116
    elements of, overview, 96–98, **98**
    Explore conversation as fluid with, 140–141
    forming and team development, 219
    giving direction with, 108–110
    giving feedback with, 110–115
    goal of, 93–94
    initiating, 116–117
    matching Inexperienced cue to, **86,** 86–87
    offering advice with, 96–102
    overview, 43–44
    providing vision with, 103–104
    sharing experience (expertise) with, 106–108
    stating expectations with, 104–106
    tribal leader example of, 93–94, 106, 108
Explore Coaching Conversation, 119–141
    case study, 129–135
    as "coaching upward," 137–138
    Coaching Wheel, overview, 51–54, **52, 53**
    conclusion arrived at by coachee in, 136–137
    Context Cone and, 73–75, **74, 75**
    Explain conversation as fluid with, 140–141
    goal of, 119–120
    initiating, 138–140
    ISEE model and, 120–129, **121, 126**
    levels of, 134
    matching Uncertain cue to, **86, 87,** 134–135
    as ongoing dialogue, 135–136
    overview, 43–44
    questions prepared for, 137
    storming and team development, 219–220
The Extraordinary Coach (Zenger and Stinnett), 6, 8–10, 96–97, 120

# F

Fazio, Rob, 28, 148
Feedback
    to encourage cooperative problem-solving, 120
    Explain Coaching Conversation for, **98**, 110–115
    following up with others for authenticity, **232**, 233
    Natural Inclination ripeness factor and, 70
Fine, Alan
    GROW model of, 10–13, 120
    You Already Know How to Be Great, 183
Five Coaching Conversations model, 43–56. *See also* Adaptability; Coaching Context; Coaching Cues; Elevate; Empower; Encourage; Evaluate "Un-Coaching" Conversation; Explain; Explore; Team development
    authenticity of, 231–234, **232**
    Best Coaches, defined, 35–42
    coaching, defined, 44–46
    Coaching Conversation, defined, 45
    Coaching Conversations Assessment, 230–231
    Coaching Wheel of, 50–54, **52, 53**
    for external coaches, 228–229
    focus as Central Issue of, 54–56, **55**
    goals of, 25–27
    intended audiences for, xvii, 223–224
    for internal leaders/coaches, 225–228
    for new coaches, 229
    organizational case study and, 48–50
    for organizations, 224–225
    overview, 43–44
    research method for, 33–42
    sports case study and, 46–48
    for tenured coaches, 230
Flavin-McDonald, Catherine, 215
Fletcher, Ryan, 137–138, 182–183

Focus, 54–56, **55**
Folkman, Joseph, 111–112

G

Gallup, 147
Gandhi, Mahatma, 24
Gardner, Howard, 27
Garvin, David, 3–4
Gates, John, 33–34, 66–67, 121, 184, 231–232
Gautama Buddha, 201
Goals, GROW model on, 10–13. *See also individual Coaching Conversations*
Goldsmith, Marshall
   Best Coach designation of, 39
   credibility of, 61
   on empowerment, 184
   on evaluating coachee, 203–204
   on question-asking paradigm, 17–18
Goleman, Daniel: *Working with Emotional Intelligence,* 27
Google, 3–4
Graddy, Jeff
   How Leaders Improve, 33–34, 66–67, 121, 184, 231–232
   Ready, Set, RIPEN!, 67
GROW (Goal, Reality, Options, Way Forward) model, 10–13, 120

H

Harvard Business Review
   "Becoming the Boss" (Hill), 59
   "Hire for Attitude" (Taylor), 212–213
   "Most Managers Don't Know How to Coach People" (Milner and Milner), 6–9
   on "Oxygen" (Google), 3–4
Heaphy, Emily, 112
Hearn, Elisabet
   Best Coach designation of, 39

on coaching cues, 84–85
on empowerment, 169, 179
Leading Teams, 135–136
Heart dimension of engagement, 215
Helping People Win at Work (Ridge and Blanchard), 93
Hersey, Paul, 24–27, 65
Herzberg, Frederick, 144–145
Hesitant cue, 86, 87–89, 222
Hesselbein, Frances, 149
Hierarchy of Needs, 144, 145
High-potential, high-performing (hi-po) employees, 26, 188–189
Hill, Linda, 59
Hippocratic Oath, 171
"Hire for Attitude" (Taylor), 212–213
"How," Empower Coaching Conversation and, 178–179, 182
How Leaders Improve (Gates, Graddy, and Lindekens), 33–34, 66–67, 121, **184,** 231–232
"How to Adopt a Coaching Mentality and Practice" (Ehrenreich and McNeely), 5
Hygiene-Motivator theory of job satisfaction, 144–145

I

"The Ideal Praise-to-Criticism Ratio" (Zenger and Folkman), 111–112
Incentive (RIPEN tool), 67–72, 202–204, 207–209
Incentives, clarifying, 158–159
Inexperienced cue, **86,** 86–87
InsideOut Development, 12
Inside-out *vs.* outside-in coaching, 13
Institute of Internal Auditors (IIA), 78
Integrative Coaching Model, 10
International Journal of Evidence Based Coaching and Mentoring, 5
ISEE (Issue, Situation, Exploration, Execution) model, 120–129
    Central Issue and, 121–122, 132–134
    for Elevate Coaching Conversation, 188
    examples, 126–129

Execution, 125–126
Exploration, 124–125
Issue, 122
question-asking techniques of, overview, 120–121
Situation, 122–124

J

Jobs, Steve, 164–165
Journal of Positive Psychology, 4
Judgment, exercising, 77–80, **79**
Jung, Carl, 21, 30–31

K

Katzenbach, Jon, 164–165
Keirsey, David, 23
Kerr, Steve, 64–66, 143–144, 171, 176
Kouzes, Jim, 59

L

Lansberg, Max, 66
Larson, Carylynn, 15
Leadership and leadership development. *See also* Five Coaching Conversations model
  coaching definition and, 45
  Leadership Inventory (Learning Bridge), 36–38, 53, 54
  leadership style of coachee, 23–27
  Social Styles model of, 16
  success indicators of leadership, 28–29
Learning Bridge, 36–38, 53, 54
Lee, Bruce, 223
Lewin, Kurt, 24
Lincoln, Abraham, 80
Lindekens, Sacha

How Leaders Improve, 33–34, 66–67, 121, 184, 231–232
Ready, Set, RIPEN!, 67
Listening
   Coaching Cues and, 84–85
   for understanding, 149–150
Losada, Marcial, 112
Loyalty, 199

M

Management of Organizational Behavior (Hersey and Blanchard), 24–27, 65
Maslow, Abraham, 144, 145
Mastery, motivation and, 145–146, 169–170, 174
Maxwell, John C., 93
McCrae, Robert, 22
McKinsey & Company, 221
McNeely, Madeleine, 5
Merrill, David, 16
Merrill, Rebecca, 10
Method. *See* Process
Milner, Julia, 6–9
Milner, Trenton, 6–9
Mindset
   adaptability of, 21–22
   fixed *vs.* growth, 160
   trust and, 8
Moen, Frode, 5
Morris, Rick, 101–102
"Most Managers Don't Know How to Coach People" (Milner and Milner), 6–9
Mother Teresa, 1
Motivation. *See also individual Coaching Conversations*
   autonomy, mastery, and purpose in, 145–146, 169–170, 174
   Hierarchy of Needs, 144, 145
   Hygiene-Motivator theory of job satisfaction, 144–145
   Motivational Currency, 148–149

for performance, 64–66, 143–144
Multiple intelligences model, 27
Multiple regression analysis, 36–37
Muscle dimension of engagement, 215
Myers-Briggs Type Indicator (MBTI), 23

N

Natural Inclination (RIPEN tool), 67–72, 202–204, 207–209
"New" cue, 22
Nightingale, Florence, 81
Noland, Kenneth, 57
Norming stage of team development, 103–104, 217–219

O

The Office (TV show), 58
Outcomes, process vs., 6–10, 18–19, 21, 48
Overall Coaching Effectiveness (Leadership Inventory, Learning Bridge), 36–38
"Oxygen" (Google), 3–4

P

Pascotto, Valerio, 8
Passmore, Jonathan, 10
Patterson, Kerry, 114
Peale, Norman Vincent, 119
Perez, Dilcie
   Best Coach designation of, 39–40
   on character, 62
   on encouragement, 160
   on explaining "why," 154
Performance. *See also* Team development
   A (ability) x M (motivation) = P (performance) formula for, 64–66, 143–144

    coaching definition and, 45
    Confidence and, 72–73
Performing stage of team development, 103-104, 217-219, 220
Personality of coachee, 22–23
Pink, Daniel, 145, 169, 174
Positive Psychology, 146–147
Positive statements, negative statements ratio, 111–112
Posner, Barry, 59
Potential. *See* Elevate Coaching Conversation
Pressley, Ayanna, 43
Pressure (RIPEN tool), 67–72, 202–204, 207–209
Process
    outcomes *vs.*, 6–10, 18–19, 21, 48
    skill needed for, 45
Professional development vs. career development and, 198
Purpose, motivation and, 145–146, 169–170, 174

Q

Question-asking paradigm of coaching, 1–19
    goals of coaching and, 3–6
    research on, 34–35
    in sports *vs.* organizational context, 1–3
    statement-making approach *vs.*, 13–19
    theories about, 6–13
Question-asking techniques
    Empowerment questions, 173–182, **182**
    Encourage Coaching Conversation and "why," 154–155
    for Explore Coaching Conversation, 133, 137

R

"Reading" others, emotional intelligence and, 28
Ready, Set, RIPEN! (Graddy and Lindekens), 67
Realization (RIPEN tool), 67–72, 202–204, 207–209
Reid, Roger, 16

Research method, 33–42
  Best Coaches identified by, 35–42
  employee engagement and, 215–216
  feedback to encourage cooperative problem-solving, 120
  goals for, 34–35
  for *How Leaders Improve* (Gates, Graddy, and Lindekens), 33–34
Retention (team development), 211, **212**, 213–214
Ridge, Garry
  Best Coach designation of, 40
  on empowerment, 173–174, 183
  on encouragement, 149
  Helping People Win at Work, 93
  tribal leader example of, 93–94, 106, 108
RIPEN (Realization, Incentive, Pressure, Expectation, Natural Inclination)
  defined, 67–72
  for Evaluate "Un-Coaching" Conversation, 202–204, 207–209
Roosevelt, Theodore, 189

S

Safety net
  empowerment and, 179
  encouragement and, 159–160
Selection (team development), 211–213, **212**
Self-actualization, 144, 145
Self-awareness
  for authenticity, **232,** 233
  emotional intelligence and, 28
Self-efficacy, 73
Self-regulation, emotional intelligence and, 28
Seligman, Martin, 146
Seppala, Emma, 146–147
The Seven Habits of Highly Effective People (Covey), 63, 149
Sinek, Simon, 154
Situation, Behavior, Impact (SBI)/Situation, Behavior, Impact, Ask (SBIA) models, 111–115
Situational Leadership model, 24–27, 65, 188

Skaalvik, Einar, 5
Skills and skillset
    adaptability of, 21–22
    matching with opportunities, 190–191
Skinner, Todd, 185
Social Styles model of leadership development, 16
Sports
    coaching case study, 46–48
    organizational context *vs.*, 1–3
Squyres, Debra
    Best Coach designation of, 40
    on coaching cues, 86
    on elevating coachee, 186–187
Stages of Team Development model (Tuckman), 103–104, 217–219. *See also* Team development
"State of the American Manager" (2017, Gallup), 147
Stein, Alan, Jr.
    Best Coach designation of, 40
    on elevating coachee, 193
Stinnett, Kathleen, 6, 8–10, 96–97, 120
Storming stage of team development, 103–104, 217–219
Strengths-Based Development, 147
Successes, celebrating, 157–158
Successful cue, 22, **86**, 89–90

T

TalentSmart, 27–28
Taylor, Bill, 212–213
Team development, 211–222
    celebrating successes with teams, 157–158
    Coaching Cues for, 222
    development, defined, 216–217
    Engagement in, 214–217
    forming and Explain approach, 219
    key factors in, 211, ***212***

norming and Encourage approach, 220
performing and Empower approach, 220
Retention in, 213–214
Selection for, 211–213
Stages of Team Development model (Tuckman), 103–104, 217–219
storming and Explore approach, 219–220
transforming and Elevate approach, 221–222
The Seven Habits of Highly Effective People (Covey), 63
The Tao of Coaching (Lansberg), 66
"The Work-Life Balance" (Morris, radio program), 101–102
Timing issues
   for Elevate Coaching Conversation, 196–197
   for Empower Coaching Conversation, 182–183
   for Encourage Coaching Conversation, 162–165
   for Explain Coaching Conversation, 116–117
   for Explore Coaching Conversation, 138–140
Transactional/Transformational leadership styles, 24
Transforming stage of team development, 221
Transparency, for authenticity, **232,** 233
Tuckman, Bruce, 103–104, 217–219
Two-factor theory of job satisfaction, 144–145
Twyman, Mike, 122–126, 158–159, 187–188

U

Uncertain cue, **86,** 87, 134–135, 222

V

Vision, providing, **98,** 103–104

W

Watson, Mary, 136–137, 178, 196–197
WD-40. *See* Ridge, Garry
"What," Empower Coaching Conversation and, 174–175, **182**
"When," Empower Coaching Conversation and, 180–181, **182**

Whitaker, Tina, 85, 87, 91

Whitmore, John, 10

"Who," Empower Coaching Conversation and, 176–178, **182**

"Why"

   Empower Coaching Conversation and, 173–174, **182**

   explaining, 154–155

"Why Coaching is a Necessary Leadership Style in a Matrix Organization" (Pascotto), 8

Wozniak, Steve, 164

Y

You Already Know How to Be Great (Fine), 12–13

Z

Zenger, John, 6, 8–10, 96–97, 111–112, 120

Think you or someone you know has what it takes to be one of our next Best Coaches?

Interested in learning more about leadership effectiveness?

Interested in participating in future Avion Consulting leadership research?

VISIT US AT

www.fivecoachingconversations.com

OR

www.avionconsulting.com